The Challenge of Establishing
World-Class Universities

The Challenge of Establishing World-Class Universities

Jamil Salmi

THE WORLD BANK
Washington, DC

1818 H Street NW
Washington DC 20433
Telephone: 202-473-1000
Internet: www.worldbank.org
E-mail: feedback@worldbank.org

ISBN: 978-0-8213-7865-6
eISBN: 978-0-8213-7876-2
DOI: 10.1596/978-0-8213-7865-6

Library of Congress Cataloging-in-Publication Data
Salmi, Jamil.
The challenge of establishing world-class universities / Jamil Salmi.
    p. cm. — (Directions in development)
    Includes bibliographical references and index.
    ISBN 978-0-8213-7865-6 (alk. paper) — ISBN 978-0-8213-7876-2
    1. Education, Higher—Economic aspects. 2. Economic development—Effect of education on. 3. Higher education and state. 4. Education and globalization. I. Title.
LC67.6.S25 2009
338.4'3378—dc22

2008051571

Cover photo: The Soochow University Library, Dushu Higher Education Town, Soochow, China, photographed by Jamil Salmi.
Cover design: Naylor Design

Contents

Boxes

Figures

Tables

Foreword

As the global environment for tertiary education expands—encompassing not only the traditional student exchanges and scholarly sojourns but also such issues as cross-border investments and market-type competition among institutions—stakeholders in tertiary education must re-evaluate their priorities and expectations. Historically, tertiary education institutions were cultural landmarks for their home nations. They educated their own students, trained their own academic staffs, and stored the cultural and local histories of their regions. International pressures, largely the result of global flows of tertiary education resources—funding, ideas, students, and staff—have forced institutions to re-examine their missions. Moreover, these pressures have forced governments, by far the largest funding sources for tertiary education, to re-examine their commitments to and expectations from their tertiary education institutions. One prominent outcome of these debates has been the rise in league tables and rankings of various sorts and, subsequently, the growing desire to compete for a place at the top of a global hierarchy of tertiary education.

The World Bank has been promoting tertiary education for development and poverty reduction since 1963. In the intervening years, the World Bank sought policy developments and innovation to encourage reforms leading to greater accessibility, equity, relevance, and quality in national tertiary education systems. Three decades into its efforts in support of tertiary education, the Bank published *Higher Education: Lessons of Experience* (1994) to frame its history and potential future endeavors regarding tertiary education. Understanding tertiary education as being more effective for development in middle-income countries, *Lessons from Experience* did not prove transformational as much as purposeful, in that its publication renewed an urgency for investing in high-quality tertiary education. In 2000, a joint UNESCO/World Bank initiative resulted in the publication of *Higher Education in Developing Countries: Perils and Promise*, further promoting the significance of tertiary education in any comprehensive development strategy. *Perils and Promise* extended the World Bank's recognition of the importance of tertiary education for comprehensive capacity building and poverty reduction, further highlighting tertiary education as a significant element within an education strategy being developed within the Bank.

The 2002 publication of *Constructing Knowledge Societies: New Challenges for Tertiary Education* underscored the fundamental importance of tertiary education in the development of globally engaged national systems, be they social, political, cultural, or economic. In order to benefit from the capacity-building potential of tertiary education, the institutions must be locally relevant yet globally engaged. The World Bank now promotes tertiary education for poverty reduction and sustainable development regardless of national income levels.

This new report, with its focus on world-class universities, examines the power of tertiary education for development from the perspective of excellence in research and scholarship at its most competitive levels. The report is extremely timely in exploring the emerging power of league tables and rankings in driving the tertiary education policy debates worldwide. In seeking a position on these lists of the best universities in the world, governments and university stakeholders have expanded their own perceptions of the purpose and position of tertiary education in the world. No longer are countries comfortable with developing their tertiary education systems to serve their local or national communities. Instead, global comparison indicators have gained significance in local development of universities. These world-class universities are now more than just cultural and educational institutions—they are points of pride and comparison among nations that view their own status in relation to other nations.

World-class standards may be a reasonable goal for some institutions in many countries, but they are likely not relevant, cost-effective, or efficient for many others. Knowing how to maneuver in this global tertiary education environment to maximize the benefits of tertiary education locally is the great challenge facing university systems worldwide. This publication is one important tool to assist with this goal.

Justin Lin
Senior Vice President and Chief Economist
The World Bank

Acknowledgments

The author wishes to express his special gratitude to Roberta Malee Bassett, who not only provided excellent research assistance but also contributed significantly to the revisions after preparation of the first draft. The author would also like to thank all the colleagues within and outside the World Bank who kindly reviewed earlier drafts and offered invaluable suggestions, in particular Nina Arnhold, Vladimir Briller, Marguerite Clarke, John Fielden, Luciano Galán, Richard Hopper, Isak Froumin, Nadia Kulikova, Yevgeny Kuznetsov, Kurt Larsen, Sam Mikhail, William Saint, Alenoush Saroyan, and Rolf Tarrach. Last but not least, Lorelei Lacdao did an excellent job of organizing and formatting the manuscript, and Veronica Grigera led the publication process in a masterful manner. The book was written under the helpful guidance of Ruth Kagia (Education Director) and Robin Horn (Education Sector Manager). Full responsibility for errors and misinterpretations remains, however, with the author.

About the Author

Jamil Salmi is the Tertiary Education Coordinator in the World Bank's Human Development Network. He was the principal author of the World Bank's most recent policy report on tertiary education reform, *Constructing Knowledge Societies: New Challenges for Tertiary Education.*

Abbreviations

AHELO	Assessing Higher Education Learning Outcomes
ARWU	Academic Ranking of World Universities
CAS	Chinese Academy of Sciences
CNRS	Centre National de la Recherche Scientifique
EIT	European Institute of Innovation and Technology
ERC	Engineering Research Centers (Republic of Korea)
FP7	Framework Programme 7 (of the European Commission)
GDP	gross domestic product
ICT	information and communication technology
IFC	International Finance Corporation (of the World Bank Group)
IITs	Indian Institutes of Technology
ITESM	Instituto Tecnológico y de Estudios Superiores de Monterrey
KOSEF	Korea Science and Engineering Foundation
LSE	London School of Economics and Political Science
MIT	Massachusetts Institute of Technology
MRC	Medical Science and Engineering Research Centers (Republic of Korea)
NCRC	National Core Research Centers (Republic of Korea)
NUS	National University of Singapore

OECD	Organisation for Economic Co-operation and Development
PPP	purchasing power parity
PSE	Paris School of Economics
SJTU	Shanghai's Jiao Tong University
SAT	Scholastic Assessment Test
SCI	Science Citation Index
SRC	Science Research Centers (Republic of Korea)
SSCI	Social Science Citation Index
SUNY	State University of New York
THES	*Times Higher Education Supplement*
UBA	University of Buenos Aires
UCLA	University of California, Los Angeles
UNAM	Universidad Nacional Autónoma de México
UNESCO	United Nations Educational, Scientific and Cultural Organization
USP	University of São Paulo
UMIST	University of Manchester Institute of Science and Technology
VUM	Victoria University of Manchester
WCU	world-class university

Executive Summary

Introduction

The ranking of world universities published by the *Times Higher Education Supplement (THES)* in September 2005 created a major controversy in Malaysia when it showed the country's top two universities slipping by almost 100 places compared with those of the previous year. Notwithstanding the fact that the big drop was mostly the result of a change in the ranking methodology—which was a little known fact and of limited comfort—the news was so traumatic that there were widespread calls for the establishment of a royal commission of inquiry to investigate the matter. A few weeks later, the Vice-Chancellor of the University of Malaya stepped down. This strong reaction was not out of character for a nation whose current Ninth Development Plan aims at shaping the transformation of the country into a knowledge-based economy, with emphasis on the important contribution of the university sector. And though apparently extreme, this reaction is not uncommon in university systems around the world.

Preoccupations about university rankings reflect the general recognition that economic growth and global competitiveness are increasingly driven by knowledge and that universities play a key role in that context. Indeed, rapid advances in science and technology across a wide range of areas—from information and communication technologies (ICTs) to biotechnology to new materials—provide great potential for countries to accelerate and strengthen their economic development. The application of knowledge results in more efficient ways of producing goods and services and delivering them more effectively and at lower costs to a greater number of people.

The 1998/99 World Development Report: Knowledge for Development (World Bank 1999a) proposed an analytical framework emphasizing the complementary role of four key strategic dimensions to guide countries in the transition to a knowledge-based economy: an appropriate economic and institutional regime, a strong human capital base, a dynamic information infrastructure, and an efficient national innovation system.

Tertiary education is central to all four pillars of this framework, but its role is particularly crucial in support of building a strong human capital base and contributing to an efficient national innovation system. Tertiary education helps countries build globally competitive economies by developing a skilled, productive, and flexible labor force and by creating, applying, and spreading new ideas and technologies. A recent global study of patent generation has shown, for example, that universities and research institutes, rather than firms, drive scientific advances in biotechnology (Cookson 2007). Tertiary education institutions can also play a vital role in their local and regional economies (Yusuf and Nabeshima 2007).

According to *Constructing Knowledge Societies*, the World Bank's latest policy report on the contribution of tertiary education to sustainable economic development (World Bank 2002), high-performing tertiary education systems encompass a wide range of institutional models—not only research universities but also polytechnics, liberal arts colleges, short-duration technical institutes, community colleges, open universities, and so forth—that together produce the variety of skilled workers and employees sought by the labor market. Each type of institution has an important role to play, and achieving a balanced development among the various components of the system is a major preoccupation of many governments. Even in a relatively advanced economy (such as Chile), the lack of prestige and quality of the nonuniversity technical education sector undermines the country's ability to meet the demands for skilled labor, as reported in a recent review of tertiary education (OECD 2009).

Within the tertiary education system, research universities play a critical role in training the professionals, high-level specialists, scientists, and researchers needed by the economy and in generating new knowledge in support of national innovation systems (World Bank 2002). In this context, an increasingly pressing priority of many governments is to make sure that their top universities are actually operating at the cutting edge of intellectual and scientific development.

There are many important questions to ask about the widespread push toward world-class status for universities around the world. Why is "world-class" the standard to which a nation should aspire to build at least a subset of its tertiary education system? Might many countries be better served by developing the most locally relevant system possible, without concern for its relative merits in a global comparison? Is the definition of "world-class" synonymous with "elite Western" and therefore inherently biased against the cultural traditions of tertiary education in non-Western countries? Are only research universities world-class, or can other types of tertiary education institutions (such as teaching universities, polytechnics, community colleges, and open universities) also aspire to be among the best of their kind in an international perspective?

This report will not delve deeply into an examination of the important questions noted above. While acknowledging that world-class universities are part of national systems of tertiary education and should operate within these systems, the main focus of this report is to explore *how* institutions become tops in their league to guide countries and university leaders seeking to achieve world-class status. The main objective of this report, therefore, is to explore the challenges involved in setting up globally competitive universities (also called "world-class," "elite," or "flagship" universities) that will be expected to compete effectively with the best of the best. Is there a pattern or template that might be followed to allow more rapid advancement to world-class status?

To answer these questions, the report starts by constructing an operational definition of a world-class university. It then outlines and analyzes possible strategies and pathways for establishing such universities and identifies the multiple challenges, costs, and risks associated with these approaches. It concludes by examining the implications of this drive for world-class institutions on the tertiary education efforts of the World Bank, offering options and alternative perspectives on how nations can develop the most effective and relevant tertiary education system to meet their specific needs.

What Does It Mean to Be a World-Class University?

In the past decade, the term "world-class university" has become a catch phrase, not simply for improving the quality of learning and research in tertiary education but also, more important, for developing the capacity to compete in the global tertiary education marketplace through the acquisition, adaptation, and creation of advanced knowledge. With students looking to attend the best possible tertiary institution that they can afford, often regardless of national borders, and with governments keen on maximizing the returns on their investments in universities, global standing is becoming an increasingly important concern for institutions around the world (Williams and Van Dyke 2007). The paradox of the world-class university, however, as Altbach has succinctly and accurately observed, is that "everyone wants one, no one knows what it is, and no one knows how to get one" (Altbach 2004).

Becoming a member of the exclusive group of world-class universities is not achieved by self-declaration; rather, elite status is conferred by the outside world on the basis of international recognition. Until recently, the process involved a subjective qualification, mostly that of reputation. For example, Ivy League universities in the United States (U.S.), such as Harvard, Yale, or Columbia; the Universities of Oxford and Cambridge in the United Kingdom (U.K.); and the University of Tokyo have traditionally been counted among the exclusive group of elite universities, but no direct and rigorous measure was available to substantiate their superior status in terms of outstanding results such as training of graduates, research output, and technology transfer. Even the higher salaries captured by their graduates could be interpreted as a signaling proxy as much as the true value of their education.

With the proliferation of league tables in the past few years, however, more systematic ways of identifying and classifying world-class universities have appeared (IHEP 2007). Although most of the best-known rankings purport to categorize universities within a given country, there have also been attempts to establish international rankings. The two most comprehensive international rankings, allowing for broad benchmark comparisons of institutions across national borders, are those prepared by the *THES* and Shanghai Jiao Tong University (SJTU).

To compare the international stature of institutions, these league tables are constructed by using objective or subjective data (or both) obtained from the universities themselves or from the public domain. The *THES* ranking selects the top 200 universities in the world. First presented in 2004, the methodology for this ranking focuses most heavily on international reputation, combining subjective inputs (such as peer reviews and employer recruiting surveys), quantitative data (including the numbers of international students and faculty), and the influence of the faculty (as represented by research citations). Operating since 2003, SJTU uses a methodology that focuses on objective indicators exclusively, such as the academic and research performance of faculty, alumni, and staff, to identify the top 500 universities in the world. The measures evaluated include publications, citations, and exclusive international awards (such as Nobel Prizes and Fields Medals). Table 1 shows the results of the 2008 *THES* and SJTU world rankings.

Notwithstanding the serious methodological limitations of any ranking exercise (Salmi and Saroyan 2007), world-class universities are recognized in part for their superior outputs. They produce well-qualified graduates who are in high demand on the labor market; they conduct leading-edge research published in top scientific journals; and in the case of science-and-technology–oriented institutions, they contribute to technical innovations through patents and licenses.

Most universities recognized as world-class originate from a very small number of countries, mostly Western. In fact, the University of Tokyo is

Table 1.   Top 20 Universities in *THES* and SJTU World Rankings, 2008

Rank	THES	Rank	SJTU
1	Harvard University	1	Harvard University
2	Yale University	2	Stanford University
3	University of Cambridge	3	University of California, Berkeley
4	University of Oxford	4	University of Cambridge
5	California Institute of Technology	5	Massachusetts Institute of Technology (MIT)
6	Imperial College London	6	California Institute of Technology
7	University College London	7	Columbia University
8	University of Chicago	8	Princeton University
9	Massachusetts Institute of Technology (MIT)	9	University of Chicago
10	Columbia University	10	University of Oxford
11	University of Pennsylvania	11	Yale University
12	Princeton University	12	Cornell University
13	Duke University	13	University of California, Los Angeles
13	Johns Hopkins University	14	University of California, San Diego
15	Cornell University	15	University of Pennsylvania
16	Australian National University	16	University of Washington, Seattle
17	Stanford University	17	University of Wisconsin, Madison
18	University of Michigan	18	University of California, San Francisco
19	University of Tokyo	19	University of Tokyo
20	McGill University	20	Johns Hopkins University

Sources: THES 2008; SJTU 2008.

the only non-U.S., non-U.K. university among the top 20 in the SJTU ranking. If one considers that there are only between 30 and 50 world-class universities in total, according to the SJTU ranking they all come from a small group of eight North American and Western European countries, Japan being again the only exception. *THES* has a slightly wider range of countries of origin among the top 50 universities (11 countries), including Hong Kong, China; New Zealand; and Singapore besides the usual North American and Western European nations (figure 1).

The few scholars who have attempted to define what world-class universities have that regular universities do not possess have identified a number of basic features, such as highly qualified faculty; excellence in research; quality teaching; high levels of government and nongovernment sources of funding; international and highly talented students; academic freedom; well-defined autonomous governance structures; and well-equipped facilities for teaching, research, administration, and (often) student life (Altbach 2004; Khoon et al. 2005; Niland 2000, 2007). Recent collaborative research on this theme between U.K. and Chinese universities (Alden and Lin 2004) has resulted in an even longer list of key attributes, ranging from the international reputation of the university to more abstract concepts such as the university's contribution to society, both very difficult to measure in an objective manner.

In an attempt to propose a more manageable definition of world-class universities, this report makes the case that the superior results of these institutions (highly sought graduates, leading-edge research, and technology

Figure 1.   Geographical Distribution of World-Class Universities
(Top 50 in 2008)

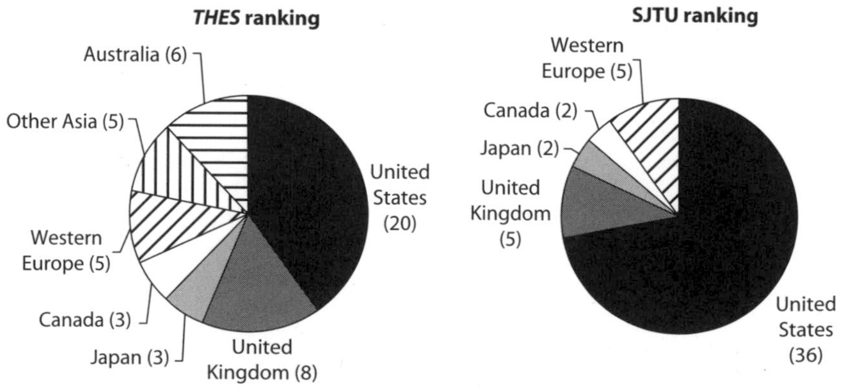

Sources: THES 2008; SJTU 2008.

transfer) can essentially be attributed to three complementary sets of factors at play in top universities: (a) a **high concentration of talent** (faculty and students), (b) **abundant resources** to offer a rich learning environment and to conduct advanced research, and (c) **favorable governance** features that encourage strategic vision, innovation, and flexibility and that enable institutions to make decisions and to manage resources without being encumbered by bureaucracy (figure 2).

Paths to Transformation

Two complementary perspectives need to be considered in examining how to establish new world-class universities. The first dimension, of an external nature, concerns the role of government at the national, state, and provincial levels and the resources that can be made available to enhance the stature of institutions. The second dimension is internal. It has to do with the individual institutions themselves and the necessary evolution and steps that they need to take to transform themselves into world-class institutions.

The Role of Government

In the past, the role of government in nurturing the growth of world-class universities was not a critical factor. The history of the Ivy League universities in the United States reveals that, by and large, they grew to prominence as a result of incremental progress, rather than by deliberate government intervention. Similarly, the Universities of Oxford and Cambridge evolved over the centuries of their own volition, with variable levels of public funding, but with considerable autonomy in terms of governance, definition of mission, and direction. Today, however, it is unlikely that a world-class university can be rapidly created without a favorable policy environment and direct public initiative and support, if only because of the high costs involved in setting up advanced research facilities and capacities.

International experience shows that three basic strategies can be followed to establish world-class universities:

- Governments could consider upgrading a small number of existing universities that have the potential of excelling (picking winners).
- Governments could encourage a number of existing institutions to merge and transform into a new university that would achieve the type of synergies corresponding to a world-class institution (hybrid formula).

Figure 2.   Characteristics of a World-Class University (WCU): Alignment of Key Factors

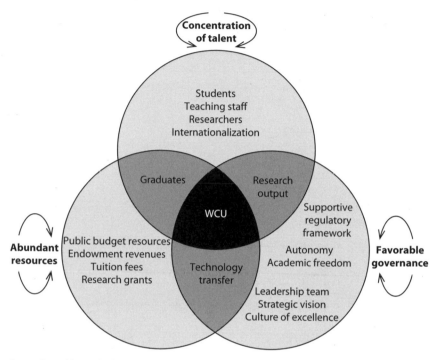

Source: Created by Jamil Salmi.

Table 2.   Costs and Benefits of Strategic Approaches for Establishing World-Class Universities

	Approach		
Conditions	Upgrading existing institutions	Merging existing institutions	Creating new institutions
Ability to attract talent	Difficult to renew staff and change the brand to attract top students	Opportunity to change the leadership and to attract new staff; existing staff may resist	Opportunity to select the best (staff and students); difficulties in recruiting top students to "unknown" institution; need to build up research and teaching traditions
Costs	Less expensive	Neutral	More expensive
Governance	Difficult to change mode of operation within same regulatory framework	More likely to work with legal status different from that of existing institutions	Opportunity to create appropriate regulatory and incentives framework
Institutional culture	Difficult to transform from within	May be difficult to create a new identity out of distinct institutional cultures	Opportunity to create culture of excellence
Change management	Major consultation and communication campaign with all stakeholders	"Normative" approach to educate all stakeholders about expected norms and institutional culture	"Environmentally adaptive" approach to communicate and socially market the new institution

Source: Created by Jamil Salmi.

- Governments could create new world-class universities from scratch (clean-slate approach).

Table 2 summarizes the pros and cons of each approach. It should be noted that these generic approaches are not mutually incompatible and that countries may pursue a combination of strategies based on these models.

Strategies at the Institutional Level
The establishment of a world-class university requires, above all, strong leadership, a bold vision of the institution's mission and goals, and a clearly articulated strategic plan to translate the vision into concrete targets and programs. Universities that aspire to better results engage in an objective

assessment of their strengths and areas for improvement, set new stretch goals, and design and implement a renewal plan that can lead to improved performance. By contrast, many institutions are complacent in their outlook, lack an ambitious vision of a better future, and continue to operate as they have in the past, ending up with a growing performance gap compared with that of their national or international competitors.

Summary Checklist

The following key questions need to be answered—by governments and institutions—to guide the quest toward establishing world-class universities:

- Why does the country need a world-class university? What is the economic rationale and the expected added value compared with the contribution of existing institutions?
- What is the vision for this university? What niche will it occupy?
- How many world-class universities are desirable and affordable as a public sector investment?
- What strategy would work best in the country context: upgrading existing institutions, merging existing institutions, or creating new institutions?
- What should be the selection process among existing institutions if the first or second approach is chosen?
- What will be the relationship and articulation between the new institution(s) and existing tertiary education institutions?
- How will the transformation be financed? What share should fall under the public budget? What share should be borne by the private sector? What incentives should be offered (for example, land grants and tax exemptions)?
- What are the governance arrangements that must be put in place to facilitate this transformation and support suitable management practices? What level of autonomy and forms of accountability will be appropriate?
- What will the government's role be in this process?
- How can the institution build the best leadership team?
- What are the vision and mission statements, and what are the specific goals that the university is seeking to achieve?
- In what niche(s) will it pursue excellence in teaching and research?
- What is the target student population?
- What are the internationalization goals that the university needs to achieve (with regard to faculty, students, programs, and so forth)?

- What is the likely cost of the proposed qualitative leap, and how is it going to be funded?
- How will success be measured? What monitoring systems, outcome indicators, and accountability mechanisms will be used?

Implications for the World Bank

In the tertiary education sector, the World Bank's work with governments in developing and transition countries has focused essentially on systemwide issues and reforms. World Bank assistance has combined policy advice, analytical work, capacity-building activities, and financial support through loans and credits to facilitate and accompany the design and implementation of major tertiary education reforms.

In recent years, however, a growing number of countries have asked the World Bank for help identifying the main obstacles preventing their universities from becoming world-class universities and mapping out ways to transform them toward this goal. To accommodate these requests, the World Bank has found that it needs to consider how to align support for individual institutions with its traditional emphasis on systemwide innovations and reforms. Experience to date suggests that this goal can be achieved through three types of complementary interventions that would be combined in a variety of configurations under different country circumstances:

- Technical assistance and guidance to assist countries in (a) identifying possible options and affordability; (b) deciding the number of elite universities that they need and can fund in a sustainable way, based on analysis guided by existing and projected financial constraints; (c) defining in each case the specific mission and niche of the institution; and (d) working out the articulation with the rest of the tertiary education system to avoid resource allocation distortions.

- Facilitation and brokering to help new elite institutions get exposure to relevant international experience through workshops and study tours. This can involve linking up with foreign partner institutions that can provide capacity-building support during the start-up years of the new institution or the transformation period of an existing institution aspiring to become world-class. The World Bank can also facilitate policy dialogue by bringing different stakeholders and partners together to agree on the vision and to garner support for the new institution(s).

- Financial support to fund preinvestment studies for the design of the project and investment costs for the actual establishment of the planned institution.

In countries that have established a positive regulatory and incentive framework to promote the development of private tertiary education, International Finance Corporation (IFC) loans and guarantees can also be used to complement or replace World Bank Group financial support if the target university or universities are set up or transformed as public–private partnerships.

It is, of course, important to tailor these options to specific country situations. Upper-middle-income countries are unlikely to be seeking financial aid as such, but are definitely looking for advice reflecting the World Bank's comparative advantage as both a knowledge broker and an observer of international experience. This advice could be provided on a fee-for-service basis.

Conclusion

The highest-ranked universities are the ones that make significant contributions to the advancement of knowledge through research, teach with the most innovative curricula and pedagogical methods under the most conducive circumstances, make research an integral component of undergraduate teaching, and produce graduates who stand out because of their success in intensely competitive arenas during their education and (more important) after graduation.

There is no universal recipe or magic formula for "making" a world-class university. National contexts and institutional models vary widely. Therefore, each country must choose, from among the various possible pathways, a strategy that plays to its strengths and resources. International experience provides a few lessons regarding the key features of such universities—high concentrations of talent, abundance of resources, and flexible governance arrangements—and successful approaches to move in that direction, from upgrading or merging existing institutions to creating new institutions altogether.

Furthermore, the transformation of the university system cannot take place in isolation. A long-term vision for creating world-class universities—and its implementation—should be closely articulated with (a) the country's overall economic and social development strategy, (b) ongoing changes and planned reforms at the lower levels of the education system, and

(c) plans for the development of other types of tertiary education institutions to build an integrated system of teaching, research, and technology-oriented institutions.

Although world-class institutions are commonly equated with top research universities, there are also world-class tertiary education institutions that are neither research focused nor operate as universities in the strictest interpretation of the term. As countries embark on the task of establishing world-class institutions, they must also consider the need to create, besides research universities, excellent alternative institutions to meet the wide range of education and training needs that the tertiary education system is expected to satisfy. The growing debate on measuring learning outcomes at the tertiary education level is testimony to the recognition that excellence is not only about achieving outstanding results with outstanding students but ought, perhaps, to be also measured in terms of how much added value is given by institutions in addressing the specific learning needs of an increasingly diverse student population.

Finally, the building pressures and momentum behind the push for world-class universities must be examined within the proper context to avoid overdramatization of the value and importance of world-class institutions and distortions in resource allocation patterns within national tertiary education systems. Even in a global knowledge economy, where every nation, both industrial and developing, is seeking to increase its share of the economic pie, the hype surrounding world-class institutions far exceeds the need and capacity for many systems to benefit from such advanced education and research opportunities, at least in the short term.

As with other service industries, not every nation needs comprehensive world-class universities, at least not while more fundamental tertiary education needs are not being met. World-class research institutions require huge financial commitments, a concentration of exceptional human capital, and governance policies that allow for top-notch teaching and research. Many nations would likely benefit from an initial focus on developing the best national universities possible, modeled perhaps on those developed as the land-grant institutions in the United States during the 19th century or the polytechnic universities of Germany and Canada. Such institutions would emphasize the diverse learning and training needs of the domestic student population and economy. Focusing efforts on the local community and economy, such institutions could lead to more effective and sustainable development than broader world-class aspirations. Regardless, institutions will inevitably, from here on out, be increasingly subject to comparisons and rankings, and those deemed to be the best in these rankings of research universities will continue be considered the very best in the world.

CHAPTER 1

What Does It Mean to Be a World-Class University?

In the past decade, the term "world-class university" has become a catch phrase, not simply for improving the quality of learning and research in tertiary education but also, more important, for developing the capacity to compete in the global tertiary education marketplace through the acquisition and creation of advanced knowledge. With students looking to attend the best possible institution that they can afford, often regardless of national borders, and with governments keen on maximizing the returns on their investments in universities, global standing is becoming an increasingly important concern for institutions around the world (Williams and Van Dyke 2007). The paradox of the world-class university, however, as Altbach has succinctly and accurately observed, is that "everyone wants one, no one knows what it is, and no one knows how to get one" (Altbach 2004).

To become a member of the exclusive group of world-class universities is not something achieved by self-declaration. This elite status is conferred by the outside world on the basis of international recognition. Until recently, the process involved a subjective qualification, mostly that of reputation. For example, Ivy League universities in the United States (U.S.), such as Harvard, Yale, or Columbia; the Universities of Oxford and Cambridge in the United Kingdom (U.K.); and the University of Tokyo have traditionally been counted among the exclusive group of elite universities, but no direct and rigorous measure was available to substantiate their superior status in terms of training of graduates, research output, and technology transfer. Even the higher salaries captured by their graduates could be interpreted as a signaling proxy as much as the true value of their education.

With the proliferation of league tables in the past few years, however, more systematic ways of identifying and classifying world-class universities have appeared (IHEP 2007). Although most of the best-known rankings purport to categorize universities within a given country, there have also been attempts to establish international rankings. The two most comprehensive international rankings, allowing for broad benchmark comparisons of institutions across national borders, are those prepared by (a) the *Times Higher Education Supplement (THES)*, produced by QS Quacquarelli Symonds Ltd., and (b) Shanghai Jiao Tong University (SJTU). A third international ranking compiled by Webometrics, produced by the Cybermetrics Lab (a unit of the National Research Council, the main public research body in Spain), compares 4,000 world tertiary education institutions and marks them on scales from 1 to 5 across several areas that purport to measure visibility on the Internet as a proxy of the importance of the concerned institution.

To compare the international stature of institutions, these league tables are constructed by using objective or subjective data (or both) obtained from the universities themselves or from the public domain. The *THES* ranking selects the top 200 universities in the world. First presented in 2004, the methodology for this ranking focuses most heavily on international reputation, combining subjective inputs (such as peer reviews and employer recruiting surveys), quantitative data (including the numbers of international students and faculty), and the influence of the faculty (as represented by research citations).

Operating since 2003, SJTU uses a methodology that focuses on seemingly more objective indicators, such as the academic and research performance of faculty, alumni, and staff. The measures evaluated include publications, citations, and exclusive international awards (such as Nobel Prizes and Fields Medals). Shanghai's ranking is also presented slightly differently: The top 100 institutions are listed in ranked ordinal. The remaining 400 institutions are listed by clusters of approximately 50 and 100 (101–52, 153–202, 203–300, and so forth) and alphabetically within those clusters. (The detailed criteria used by each of the three world rankings are presented in appendix A.) Table 1.1 shows the results of the 2008 SJTU and *THES* world rankings.

Notwithstanding the serious methodological limitations of any ranking exercise summarized in box 1.1, world-class universities are recognized in part for their superior outputs. They produce well-qualified graduates who are in high demand on the labor market; they conduct leading-edge research published in top scientific journals; and in the case of science-and-technology–oriented institutions, they contribute to technical innovations through patents and licenses.

Most universities recognized as world-class originate from a very small number of countries, mostly Western. In fact, the University of Tokyo is the only non-U.S., non-U.K. university among the top 20 in the SJTU ranking. If one considers that there are only between 30 and 50 world-class universities in total, according to the SJTU ranking

Table 1.1.   Top 20 Universities in *THES* and SJTU World Rankings, 2008

Rank	THES	Rank	SJTU
1	Harvard University	1	Harvard University
2	Yale University	2	Stanford University
3	University of Cambridge	3	University of California, Berkeley
4	University of Oxford	4	University of Cambridge
5	California Institute of Technology	5	Massachusetts Institute of Technology (MIT)
6	Imperial College London	6	California Institute of Technology
7	University College London	7	Columbia University
8	University of Chicago	8	Princeton University
9	Massachusetts Institute of Technology (MIT)	9	University of Chicago
10	Columbia University	10	University of Oxford
11	University of Pennsylvania	11	Yale University
12	Princeton University	12	Cornell University
13	Duke University	13	University of California, Los Angeles
13	Johns Hopkins University	14	University of California, San Diego
15	Cornell University	15	University of Pennsylvania
16	Australian National University	16	University of Washington, Seattle
17	Stanford University	17	University of Wisconsin, Madison
18	University of Michigan	18	University of California, San Francisco
19	University of Tokyo	19	University of Tokyo
20	McGill University	20	Johns Hopkins University

Sources: THES 2008; SJTU 2008.

Box 1.1

Understanding and Using Rankings to Their Best Advantage

Just as scarcity, prestige, and having access to "the best" increasingly mark the purchase of goods such as cars, handbags, and blue jeans, the consumers of tertiary education are also looking for indicators that enhance their capacity to identify and access the best universities. In this race for "luxury" education, countries are striving to develop "world-class universities" that will spearhead the development of a knowledge-based economy. Because of the power of rankings, institutions are playing a game of innovating and investing in light of ranking methodologies, perhaps at the expense of their real strengths, financial capabilities, and institutional capacity.

Regardless of their controversial nature and methodological shortcomings, university rankings have become widespread and are unlikely to disappear. Because they define what "world-class" is to the broadest audience, they cannot be ignored by anyone interested in measuring the performance of tertiary education institutions. The following general recommendations, developed out of a recent analysis of league tables, may help clarify for policy makers, administrators, and users of tertiary education how to determine the real value of the educational opportunity offered by an institution:

- Be clear about what the ranking actually measures.
- Use a range of indicators and multiple measures, rather than a single, weighted ranking.
- Consumers should be aware of comparing similar programs or institutions.
- Institutions can use rankings for strategic planning and quality improvement purposes.
- Governments can use rankings to stimulate a culture of quality.
- Consumers of the rankings data can use the rankings as one of the instruments available to inform students, families, and employers and to fuel public debates.

Source: Salmi and Saroyan 2007.

they all come from a small group of eight North American and Western European countries, Japan being again the only exception (appendix B). *THES* has a slightly wider range of countries of origin among the top 50 universities (11 countries), including Hong Kong (China), New Zealand, and Singapore besides the usual North American and

Western European nations (appendix C). Figure 1.1 shows the broad geographical distribution of the countries whose universities appear among the top 50 in the world rankings.

The few scholars who have attempted to define what world-class universities have that regular universities do not possess have identified a number of basic features, such as highly qualified faculty; excellence in research; quality teaching; high levels of government and nongovernment sources of funding; international and highly talented students; academic freedom; well-defined autonomous governance structures; and well-equipped facilities for teaching, research, administration, and (often) student life (Altbach 2004; Khoon et al. 2005; Niland 2000, 2007). Recent collaborative research on this theme between U.K. and Chinese universities (Alden and Lin 2004) has resulted in an even longer list of key attributes, ranging from the international reputation of the university to more abstract concepts such as the university's contribution to society, both very difficult to measure in an objective manner (appendix D).

In an attempt to propose a more manageable definition of world-class universities, this report makes the case that the superior results of these institutions (highly sought graduates, leading-edge research, and technology transfer) can essentially be attributed to three complementary sets of factors at play in top universities: (a) a **high concentration of talent** (faculty and students), (b) **abundant resources** to offer a rich learning

Figure 1.1.   Geographical Distribution of World-Class Universities
(Top 50 in 2008)

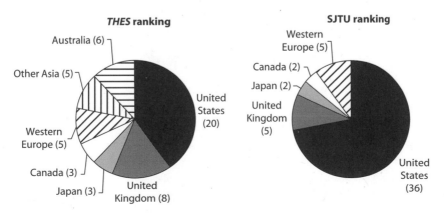

Source: THES 2008; SJTU 2008.

environment and to conduct advanced research, and (c) **favorable governance** features that encourage strategic vision, innovation, and flexibility and that enable institutions to make decisions and to manage resources without being encumbered by bureaucracy.

Concentration of Talent

The first and perhaps foremost determinant of excellence is the presence of a critical mass of top students and outstanding faculty. World-class universities are able to select the best students and attract the most qualified professors and researchers.

> In the sciences, being at the right university—the one where the most state-of-the-art research is being done in the best-equipped labs by the most visible scientists—is extremely important. George Stigler describes this as a snowballing process, where an outstanding scientist gets funded to do exciting research, attracts other faculty, then the best students—until a critical mass is formed that has an irresistible appeal to any young person entering the field.
>
> Mihaly Csikszentmihalyi (1997)

This has always been the hallmark of the Ivy League universities in the United States or the Universities of Oxford and Cambridge in the United Kingdom. And it is also a feature of the newer world-class universities, such as the National University of Singapore (NUS) or Tsinghua University in China.

> Beijing's Tsinghua University said last month it would increase the number of awards this year. Students with high scores, such as champions of each province and winners of international student academic competitions, will be entitled to scholarships of up to 40,000 yuan ($5,700), more than double that of last year.
>
> *University World News (UWN)* (2008a)

Important factors in that respect are the ability and the privilege of these universities to select the most academically qualified students. For example, Beijing University, China's top institution of higher learning, admits the 50 best students of each province every year. Harvard University, the California Institute of Technology, the Massachusetts Institute of Technology (MIT), and Yale University are the most selective universities in the United States, as measured by the average Scholastic Assessment Test (SAT) scores of their incoming undergraduate students.

One corollary of this observation is that tertiary education institutions in countries where there is little internal mobility of students and faculty are at risk of academic inbreeding. Indeed, universities that rely principally on their own undergraduates to continue into graduate programs or that hire principally their own graduates to join the teaching staff are not likely to be at the leading edge of intellectual development. A 2007 survey of European universities found an inverse correlation between endogamy in faculty hiring and research performance: the universities with the highest degree of endogamy had the lowest research results (Aghion et al. 2008).

It is also difficult to maintain high selectivity in institutions with rapidly growing student enrollment and fairly open admission policies. The huge size of the leading universities of Latin American countries such as Mexico or Argentina—the Universidad Nacional Autónoma de México (Autonomous University of Mexico, or UNAM) has 190,418 students, and the University of Buenos Aires (UBA) has 279,306—is certainly a major factor in explaining why these universities have failed to enter the top league, despite having a few excellent departments and research centers that are undoubtedly world-class. At the other extreme, Beijing University maintained its overall enrollment at less than 20,000 until the early 2000s and even today has no more than 30,000 students.

World-class universities also tend to have a high proportion of carefully selected graduate students (as illustrated by table 1.2), reflecting their strength in research and the fact that graduate students are closely involved in the research activities of these institutions.

The international dimension is becoming increasingly important in determining the configuration of these elite institutions (box 1.2). Both the *THES* world ranking of universities and the *Newsweek* 2006 ranking of global universities weighted their rankings to favor institutions with strong international components. In most cases, world-class universities have students and faculty who are not exclusively from the country where the university operates. This enables them to attract the most talented people, no matter where they come from, and open themselves to new ideas and approaches. Harvard University, for instance, has a student population that is 19 percent international; Stanford University has 21 percent; and Columbia University, 23 percent. At the University of Cambridge, 18 percent of the students are from outside the U.K. or European Union (EU) countries. The U.S. universities ranked at the top of the global surveys also show sizable proportions of foreign academic staff. For example, the proportion of international faculty at Harvard University, including medical

Table 1.2.   Weight of Graduate Students in Selected Universities

University	Undergraduate students	Graduate students	Share of graduate students (percentage)
Harvard[a]	7,002	10,094	59
Stanford[b]	6,442	11,325	64
MIT[c]	4,066	6,140	60
Oxford[d]	11,106	6,601	37
Cambridge[e]	12,284	6,649	35
London School of Economics and Political Science (LSE)[f]	4,254	4,386	51
Beijing[g]	14,662	16,666	53
Tokyo[h]	15,466	12,676	45

a. 2005–06 http://vpf-web.harvard.edu/budget/factbook/current_facts/2006OnlineFactBook.pdf.
b. 2006–07 http://www.stanford.edu/home/statistics/#enrollment.
c. 2005–06 http://web.mit.edu/ir/cds/2006/b.html.
d. 2005–06 http://www.ox.ac.uk/aboutoxford/annualreview/app2ii.shtml.
e. 2004–05 http://www.admin.cam.ac.uk/reporter/2004-05/special/19/studentnumbers2005.pdf.
f. Kahn and Malingre 2007.
g. 2006–07 Beijing University Admission Office.
h. 2004 http://www.u-tokyo.ac.jp/stu04/e08_02_e.html.

Box 1.2

The Best of Both Worlds at the University of Oxford

The University of Oxford has nominated the Provost of Yale University, Professor Andrew Hamilton, as its next vice-chancellor. Provided the university dons approve the appointment, Hamilton will replace the current vice-chancellor, Dr. John Hood, who retires next year after his five-year appointment ends.

He is one of the few academics to be appointed to head Oxford who did not graduate from the university and is only the second—after Hood, who came from New Zealand—to be recruited from outside.

His appointment follows Oxford's announcement last month of a massive fundraising campaign of 1.25 billion pounds (£1.25 billion, or US$2.5 billion) to attract the world's top academics, of whom the university clearly considers Hamilton to be one.

Oxford Chancellor Lord Patten chaired the nominating committee and said that Hamilton had a remarkable combination of proven academic leadership and outstanding scholarly achievement "that makes him an exceptional choice to help guide us into the second decade of the 21st century."

Source: UWN 2008b.

academic staff, is approximately 30 percent. Similarly, the proportion of foreign academics at the Universities of Oxford and Cambridge is 36 and 33 percent, respectively. By contrast, only 7 percent of all researchers in France are foreign academics. Unquestionably, the world's best universities enroll and employ large numbers of foreign students and faculty in their search for the most talented.

The new patterns of knowledge generation and sharing, documented by Gibbons et al. (1994) in their groundbreaking work on the shift toward a problem-based mode of production of knowledge, are characterized by the growing importance of international knowledge networks. In this respect, the fact that world-class universities succeed in mobilizing a broadly diverse national and international academic staff is likely to maximize these institutions' knowledge-networking capacity.

Abundant Resources

Abundance of resources is the second element that characterizes most world-class universities, in response to the huge costs involved in running a complex, research-intensive university. These universities have four main sources of financing: government budget funding for operational expenditures and research, contract research from public organizations and private firms, the financial returns generated by endowments and gifts, and tuition fees.

In Western Europe, public funding is by far the principal source of finance for teaching and research, although the top U.K. universities have some endowment funds, and "top-up fees" have been introduced in recent years. In Asia, the National University of Singapore, which became a private corporation in 2006, has been the most successful institution in terms of substantial endowment funding. It has managed to build up a sizable portfolio of US$774 million through effective fund-raising, making it richer than any British university after Cambridge and Oxford. The United States and (to a lesser extent) Japan have thriving private research universities.

The sound financial base of the top U.S. universities is the result of two factors. First, they have large endowments (table 1.3), which provide budget security, comfort, and the ability to focus on medium- and long-term institutional priorities. On average, per student, the richest U.S. private universities receive more than US$40,000 in endowment income every year, compared with a mere US$1,000 for Canadian universities (Usher and Savino 2006). Unlike many universities in Europe, these U.S. universities are not at the short-term mercy of government funding

Table 1.3.   Comparison of U.S. and U.K. Endowment Levels

U.S. institutions	Endowment assets (2006, US$ millions)	U.K. institutions	Endowment assets (2005, US$ millions)
Harvard University	28,916	University of Cambridge	6,100
Yale University	18,031	University of Oxford	3,800
Stanford University	14,085	University of Edinburgh	3,400
University of Texas	13,235	University of Glasgow	230
Princeton University	13,045	King's College London	200

Source: NACUBO 2006.
Note: US$1 = £.53

sources or the whims of changing political priorities. Moreover, as their prestige increases, so does their ability to attract donations, as evidenced by a study of the positive correlation between ranking and the size of a university's endowment (Monks and Ehrenberg 1999).

Second, U.S. universities benefit from the success of their faculty in competing for government research funding. At least two-thirds of the research funding captured by the top U.S. research universities comes from public sources. The top-ranking Canadian universities in international league tables are also the top universities in research income (Salmi and Saroyan 2007).

A comparative analysis of the SJTU rankings of U.S. and Western European universities confirms that level of expenditures is one of the key determinants of performance. Total spending on tertiary education (public and private) represents 3.3 percent of gross domestic product (GDP) in the United States versus only 1.3 percent in the EU25 countries. Per student spending is about US$54,000 in the United States, compared with US$13,500 in the European Union (Aghion et al. 2008). Similarly, there are large spending variations among European universities that are correlated with the rankings results of the respective countries. The United Kingdom and Switzerland have relatively well-funded universities and achieve the highest country scores in terms of rankings, while universities from the Southern European countries, including France and Germany, have lower ranking scores associated with low levels of funding (Aghion et al. 2007).

The availability of abundant resources creates a virtuous circle that allows the concerned institutions to attract even more top professors and researchers, as is often the case among elite universities in the United States. Annual surveys of salaries indicate that private universities in the

United States pay their professors 30 percent more than public universities do, on average. The salary gap between public and private universities has increased in the past 25 years. In 1980, the average salary of full professors at doctor-of-philosophy (PhD)–granting public universities amounted to 91 percent of that at private universities. Today, the US$106,500 average annual salary at public universities represents 78 percent of the salary at private universities (*Chronicle of Higher Education [CHE]* 2007). It is not surprising, then, that not one U.S. public institution ranks nationally in the top 20 (*U.S. News* & *World Report* 2009); private universities reward excellent faculty with higher salaries, so the best academics tend to seek employment there. A recent article on the University of Wisconsin (box 1.3)

Box 1.3

Impact of the Talent War on the University of Wisconsin

Jon C. Pevehouse had not even finished his first year as a tenure-track professor at the University of Wisconsin at Madison in 2001 when other universities began trying to lure him away. By last year, Mr. Pevehouse decided it was time to consider the offers seriously. He quickly ended up more than doubling his salary, with a move to the University of Chicago. . . .

The problem is money. Wisconsin's stagnating state higher-education budget has forced the university to keep faculty salaries far below average. When professors get feelers from elsewhere, they learn that a move can easily mean a whopping 100 percent salary increase—sometimes more. . . .

Some people worry that the wave of faculty departures is damaging Madison's reputation as a premier public institution. From 2006 to 2007, the university dropped from No. 34 to No. 38 in *U.S. News & World Report*'s rankings of national doctoral institutions. . . .

About 400 professors at Madison received job offers from other colleges in the past four years. That is double the number who received offers in the four years before that. While in some years the university has been able to hang on to as many as 80 percent of those with outside offers, the proportion slipped to 63 percent last year. . . .

Faculty turnover is expensive. Overall, across the disciplines, Madison figures that it spends an average of $1.2 million in start-up costs for each new professor. It typically takes eight years for a professor to bring in enough research money to cover that cost. A professor who stays at Madison for 25 years after earning tenure brings in an average of about $13 million in research money. But the university loses many professors before they even pay off the initial investment.

Source: Wilson 2008.

documented how years of scarce funding led to the loss of significant numbers of top faculty "raided" by other institutions and a drop in its national rankings (CHE 2008).

Table 1.4 shows pay averages regarding researcher salaries across the EU and a few comparator countries. As one would expect, salaries in countries with the highest numbers of institutions on the world rankings of tertiary education are the highest, while countries with little or no global tertiary education presence have the lowest salaries. It must not be mistaken as a coincidence that the best-quality research appears to be coming out of the best-paid researcher pools. In academia, the adage "you get what you pay for" appears accurate regarding better-quality work being done where salaries are relatively highest.

In the United States, an even larger remuneration gap between private and public institutions is prevalent when it comes to the pay packages of university presidents (as illustrated by table 1.5, which compares the top three best-paid presidents of both types of institutions).

The resource gap affects, in turn, the financial capacity of countries to put in place the kind of digital infrastructure enjoyed by top universities in North America and East Asia. A recent report on French universities, for example, underscores the need to catch up with more-advanced tertiary education systems, which explains the poor showing of French universities in the Webometrics rankings. In the words of the Minister of Education,

> In the context of globalization of higher education, it appears that France shows a certain delay compared with other Western countries in the access it provides to online courses and in offering distance education. At the very time when mastering information and communication technologies seems increasingly to be an element of a nation's competitiveness, this delay in the digitization of higher studies risks impeding France's development in coming years.
>
> Marshall (2008)

Appropriate Governance

The third dimension concerns the overall regulatory framework, the competitive environment, and the degree of academic and managerial autonomy that universities enjoy. The *Economist* (2005) referred to the tertiary education system in the United States as "the best in the world" and attributed this success not only to its wealth but also to its relative independence from the state, the competitive spirit that encompasses

Table 1.4.   International Comparison of Average Salaries of Researchers

(Total Yearly Salary Average of Researchers in EU25, Associated Countries, Australia, China, India, Japan, and the United States [2006, N=6110, all currencies in euros and in terms of PPPs])

	Remuneration average in euros	Corrective coefficient	Remuneration average in terms of PPPs
Austria	62.406	103.1	60.530
Belgium	58.462	104.4	55.998
Cyprus	45.039	89.1	50.549
Czech Republic	19.620	53.1	36.950
Denmark	61.355	140.5	43.669
Estonia	11.748	55.8	21.053
Finland	44.635	121.8	36.646
France	50.879	107.0	47.550
Germany	56.132	105.2	53.358
Greece	25.685	83.3	30.835
Hungary	15.812	57.1	27.692
Ireland	60.727	122.3	49.654
Italy	36.201	106.1	34.120
Latvia	10.488	48.6	21.580
Lithuania	13.851	46.7	29.660
Luxembourg	63.865	113.5	56.268
Malta	28.078	69.6	40.342
Netherlands	59.103	104.2	56.721
Poland	11.659	54.0	21.591
Portugal	29.001	87.0	33.334
Slovakia	9.178	50.2	18.282
Slovenia	27.756	73.1	37.970
Spain	34.908	89.8	38.873
Sweden	56.053	118.9	47.143
United Kingdom	56.048	106.2	52.776
EU25 average	*37.948 €*		*40.126€*
Bulgaria	3.556	36.4	9.770
Croatia	16.671	61.6	27.063
Iceland	50.803	150.3	33.801
Israel (*)	42.552	71.4	59.580
Norway	58.997	141.1	41.813
Romania	6 286	46.6	13.489
Switzerland	B2.72S	138.1	59.902
Turkey	16.249	61.9	26.250
Associated countries average	*34. 730 €*		*33.959€*
Australia(*)	64.150	102.9	62 342
China(*)	3.150	22.9	13.755
India(*)	9.177	20.3	45.207
Japan	68.872	111.1	61.991
United States	60.156	95.8	62 793

Source: EC 2007, 19.

* The corrective coefficients in those countries are the purchasing power parity (PPP) published by the World Bank. PPP is expressed as the local currency unit to the international dollar.

Table 1.5.   Annual Compensation: Highest Paid U.S. University Presidents, 2005–06

Private universities	Total compensation (US$)	Public universities	Total compensation (US$)
Northeastern University	2,887,800	University of Delaware	874,700
Philadelphia University	2,557,200	University of Virginia	753,700
Johns Hopkins University	1,938,000	University of Washington	752,700

Source: CHE 2007.

every aspect of it, and its ability to make academic work and production relevant and useful to society. The report observed that the environment in which universities operate fosters competitiveness, unrestrained scientific inquiry, critical thinking, innovation, and creativity. Moreover, institutions that have complete autonomy are also more flexible because they are not bound by cumbersome bureaucracies and externally imposed standards, even in light of the legitimate accountability mechanisms that do bind them. As a result, they can manage their resources with agility and quickly respond to the demands of a rapidly changing global market.

The comparative study of European and U.S. universities mentioned earlier also found that governance was, along with funding, the other main determinant of rankings. "European universities suffer from poor governance, insufficient autonomy and often perverse incentives" (Aghion et al. 2007, 1). A subsequent paper reporting on a survey of European universities found that research performance was positively linked to the degree of autonomy of the universities in the sample, especially with regard to budget management, the ability to hire faculty and staff, and the freedom to set salaries (Aghion et al. 2008). With respect to the composition of university boards, the report concludes that "having significant outside representation on the board may be a necessary condition to ensure that dynamic reforms taking into account long-term institutional interests can be decided upon without undue delay."

The autonomy elements outlined above are necessary, though not sufficient, to establish and maintain world-class universities. Other crucial governance features are needed, such as inspiring and persistent leaders; a strong strategic vision of where the institution is going; a philosophy of success and excellence; and a culture of constant reflection, organizational learning, and change.

The cases of Germany and France are interesting to discuss in this context. Despite having economies that are among the strongest in the world, their universities are hardly recognized as elite institutions. In 2003, when the first SJTU ranking was published, the best French university (the University of Paris VI) was ranked 66th, and the first German university (the University of Munich) was ranked 49th. In 2008, the best French and German universities were placed 42nd and 55th, respectively.

Benchmarking them against the three sets of criteria proposed above shows clearly why universities of these two countries do not shine in international rankings. To begin with, there is very little screening of students entering tertiary education. By law, French universities are not allowed to be selective. In most programs, having graduated from secondary school is the only prerequisite to admission, with the exception of the highly selective French engineering and professional *grandes écoles*, which have a separate status.

Another important factor is the absolute lack of competition among universities. All universities are treated equally in terms of budget and assignment of personnel, making it quite difficult, if not impossible, to mobilize the necessary resources to set up centers of excellence with a large concentration of top researchers. For both Germany and France, per student public expenditures on tertiary education are slightly below the Organisation for Economic Co-operation and Development (OECD) average and are half the level of U.S. universities. When the first SJTU ranking was published at the end of 2003, the daily paper *Le Monde* ran an article on January 24, 2004, entitled "The Great Misery of French Universities." The university presidents and union leaders interviewed for that article argued that the lack of budgetary resources and the rigidities associated with their utilization were the main explanations for the demise of the French university system.

Finally, in both countries, universities are government entities constrained by civil service employment rules and rigid management controls. This means, in particular, that it is not possible to pay higher salaries to reward the more productive academics or to attract world-class researchers or to invest in leading-edge research facilities. For example, the salaries of French business administration professors are 20 percent lower than those of their U.S. counterparts (Egide 2007). Commenting on the 2005 initiative of the European Union to create a European Institute of Innovation and Technology (EIT) after the MIT model, the scientific magazine *Nature* noted in a March 2008 editorial that

. . . the very existence of the EIT concept—and its survival through the rough seas of EU politics—is an indictment of Europe's suffocating national bureaucracies, which have made it impossible for universities and publicly funded research institutes to evolve into MITs on their own. "Elite" has too often been treated as a dirty word, and interactions with industry considered a betrayal of academic purity. In many countries, including France, Germany and Italy, it is still generally impossible to offer internationally competitive packages for top researchers. . . .

The EIT may yet surprise its critics. Either way, national efforts to boost universities are by far the best way to address the problems that the EIT is intended to solve.

Nature (2008)

In the case of France, two additional structural features complicate the situation further. First, according to Orivel (2004), one of the main reasons why French universities are not internationally competitive is the dual structure of the tertiary education system (box 1.4). The top engineering and professional schools (*grandes écoles*) recruit the best students through very competitive national examinations, while the universities receive the bulk of secondary school graduates who have automatic access. Because the *grandes écoles* are predominantly elite, professionally oriented schools, they conduct very little research; as a result, most doctoral students in the research universities do not come from the most academically qualified student groups. This is quite unlike the practice in more competitive university systems in the United States, the United

---

Box 1.4

Watching the Rankings: The French Experience

Each year, when Shanghai's Jiao Tong University publishes its world ranking of universities, France responds with a mix of indignation and consternation. Indignation, because French educators complain that the system favors "Anglo-Saxon" universities and makes no allowance for France's unusual division into elite *grandes écoles* and mass universities. Consternation, because not a single French university makes it into the world's top 40. Its best-placed institution—Paris VI— manages only 45th place.

Source: Economist 2006.

Kingdom, or Japan. Second, the strict separation between the research institutes affiliated with the Centre National de la Recherche Scientifique (the National Center for Scientific Research, or CNRS) and the research departments of the universities results in the dispersion of human and financial resources. The strength of world-class universities is that research is usually integrated at all levels.

Alignment of Success Factors

Finally, it is important to stress that it is the combination of these three sets of features—concentration of talent, abundant funding, and appropriate governance—that makes the difference. The dynamic interaction among these three groups of factors is the distinguishing characteristic of high-ranking universities (as illustrated by figure 1.2).

The results of the recent survey of European universities confirm that funding and governance influence performance together. They indicate clearly that the higher-ranked universities tend to enjoy increased management autonomy, which, in turn, increases the efficiency of spending and results in higher research productivity.

> But our main result is not simply that more money or more autonomy is good for research performance. It is that more money has much more impact when it is combined with budget autonomy. To be more precise: we find that having budget autonomy doubles the effect of additional money on university research performance.
>
> Aghion et al. (2008)

Having an appropriate governance framework without sufficient resources or the ability to attract top talent does not work either. Similarly, just investing money in an institution or making it very selective in terms of student admission is not sufficient to build a world-class university, as illustrated by the case of Brazil's top university, the University of São Paulo (USP). Brazil is the 5th most populated nation and the 10th largest economy on the planet, it is among the six largest producers of cars in the world, it has world-class companies such as Embraer and Aracruz Celulose, but there is no Brazilian university among the 100 top-ranked universities in the world.

How is it that USP, the country's foremost university, does not make it into the top group in the international rankings, despite having some of the features of world-class universities? When it was created in 1934, the USP founders and first leaders made it a point to hire only prominent

Figure 1.2.   Characteristics of a World-Class University (WCU): Alignment of Key Factors

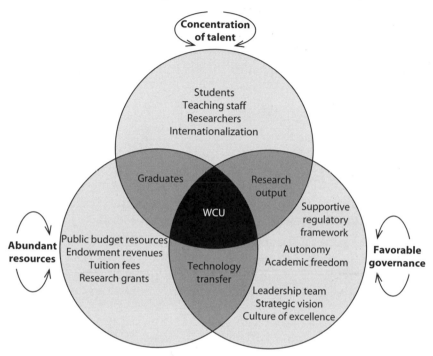

Source: Created by Jamil Salmi.

professors from all over Europe (Schwartzman 2005). Today, it is the most selective institution in Brazil, it has the highest number of top-rated graduate programs, and every year it produces more PhD graduates than any U.S. university.

At the same time, USP's ability to manage its resources is constrained by rigid civil service regulations, even though it is the richest university in the country. Added to this is the fact that, at USP as in other Brazilian universities, the spirit of democracy has translated into multiple representative bodies (*assembleas*) which complicates decision making and the implementation of any forward-looking reform (Durham 2008). USP has very few linkages with the international research community, and only 3 percent of its graduate students are from outside Brazil. The university is very inward looking: most students come from the state of São Paulo, and the majority of professors are USP graduates (this latter feature of endogamy being a typical feature of European universities, as

Table 1.6.   Ranking of Universities Where Professors Earn Most

University	Average annual salary of full professors, 2007–08 (US$)	Shanghai Jiao Tong University ranking, 2008
Rockefeller University	191,200	32
Harvard University	184,800	1
Stanford University	173,700	2
Princeton University	172,200	8
University of Chicago	170,800	9
Yale University	165,100	11
University of Pennsylvania	163,300	15
Columbia University	162,500	7
New York University	162,400	31
California Institute of Technology	162,200	6
Northwestern University	153,600	30
Massachusetts Institute of Technology (MIT)	151,600	5
Washington University in St. Louis	150,800	29
Boston College	149,300	Not among 100 top
Cornell University	148,200	12
Dartmouth College	147,800	Not among 100 top
Emory University	147,200	Not among 100 top
University of Maryland, Baltimore	142,700	Not among 100 top
University of Southern California	140,100	50
New Jersey Institute of Technology	139,500	Not among 100 top

Source: CHE 2007.

discussed earlier). Foreign students are forbidden to write a doctoral dissertation in a language other than Portuguese. According to Schwartzman (2005), the key missing element is the absence of a vision of excellence to challenge the status quo and transform the university. The lack of ambitious strategic vision can be observed as much at the national and state government levels as among the university leadership.

Financial resources data from the United States confirm that money alone is not a guarantee of excellence in teaching and research. The top U.S. universities in the world rankings all have abundant resources, but some universities with equally high spending levels achieve significantly lower results (as illustrated by table 1.6, on page 33, which shows the Shanghai Jiao Tong ranking of the top 20 universities with the highest-paid full professors).[1]

Along the same lines, it is interesting to note that among the five most expensive U.S. four-year institutions in terms of levels of tuition fees charged—George Washington University, Kenyon College, Bucknell University, Vassar College, and Sarah Lawrence College—only the first one is a research university, and it is not among the top 100 universities in the SJTU ranking of world universities.

---

1 It is important to nuance this analysis by recognizing the influence of institutional context factors. Salary averages may be skewed by the presence of medical, business, and law faculties, for whom the pay tends to be higher than in the arts and sciences. Rockefeller University, in particular, is entirely a medical university, which impacts both the pay averages and the indicators for SJTU, which are better served by greater disciplinary diversity.

CHAPTER 2

Paths to Transformation

Infosys and Wipro are great role models. I cannot say that I will be as great as them, but today India is producing more entrepreneurs than any other country. . . . As chairman of Jet Airways, I definitely would like to see India able to create a world-class airline. We should not be inferior to Singapore and Cathay Pacific in terms of reliability and standards of service. We will hire the best brains, the best talent. We aim to be second to none.

Naresh Goyal, Jet Airways Founder and Chairman
Newsweek interview, July 16, 2007

Two complementary perspectives need to be considered in examining how to establish new world-class universities. The first dimension, of an external nature, concerns the role of government at the national, state, and provincial levels and the resources that can be made available to enhance the stature of institutions. The second dimension is internal. It has to do with the individual institutions themselves and the necessary evolution and steps that they need to take to transform themselves into world-class institutions.

The Role of Government

In the past, the role of government in nurturing the growth of world-class universities was not a critical factor. The history of the Ivy League universities in the United States reveals that, by and large, they grew to prominence as a result of incremental progress, rather than by deliberate government intervention. Similarly, the Universities of Oxford and Cambridge evolved over the centuries of their own volition, with variable levels of public funding, but with considerable autonomy in terms of governance, definition of mission, and direction. Today, however, it is unlikely that a world-class university can be rapidly created without a favorable policy environment and direct public initiative and support, if only because of the high costs involved in setting up advanced research facilities and capacities.

Altbach (2004) reports a late-19th-century conversation between John D. Rockefeller and the then-President of Harvard University, Charles W. Eliot, in which Rockefeller asked Eliot what would be the cost of establishing a world-class university. Eliot's answer was "50 million dollars and 200 years." However, the University of Chicago was able, at the beginning of the 20th century, to achieve this goal within only 20 years, although the price tag at that time was already more than US$100 million.

Professor Altbach estimates the cost of creating a world-class university today to be around US$500 million, and, indeed, the actual cost would very likely be much higher. The School of Medicine established by Cornell University in Qatar in 2002 cost alone US$750 million (Mangan 2008). The government of Pakistan is planning to spend US$700 million for each of the new Universities of Engineering, Science, and Technology that it is planning to create in the next few years.

In that respect, some of the key questions that national authorities need to ponder is how many—if any—world-class universities their country can afford and how to make sure that investment for that purpose will not come at the expense of investing in other priority areas in the tertiary education sector. Adopting the goal of building world-class universities does not imply, however, that all universities in a given country can be or should aspire to be of international standing. A more attainable and appropriate goal would be, rather, to develop an integrated system of teaching, research, and technology-oriented institutions that feed into and support a few centers of excellence that focus on value-added fields and chosen areas of comparative advantage and that can eventually evolve into world-class institutions.

The California higher-education master plan, formulated in the early 1960s, is a good example of strategic vision translated into a highly diversified system (box 2.1). The California system of higher education integrates and supports a broad array of tertiary education institutions, which are connected through administrative and academic bridges and clear recognition rules. Today, California boasts 474 tertiary education institutions: 145 public universities, 109 private universities, and the remaining institutions divided between community colleges and vocationally oriented institutes. Out of these, two private universities (Stanford University and the California Institute of Technology) and four public universities (the Universities of California at Berkeley, Los Angeles, San Diego, and San Francisco) are among the top 20 universities in the SJTU ranking.

Box 2.1

Setting the Policy Framework for Higher Education in California

California pioneered the establishment of a policy framework for a state system of higher education in the United States when it developed and implemented its first Master Plan in 1959–60. The primary issues considered at that time were the future roles of the public and private sectors and, in particular, how the public sector should be governed and coordinated to avoid duplication and waste. Major principles that emerged from the initial Master Plan still shape the state's system today:

- Recognition of different missions for the four components of the higher-education system (Universities of California, California State Universities, community colleges, and private universities and junior colleges)
- Establishment of a statutory coordinating body for the entire system
- Differential admission pools for the state universities and colleges
- Eligibility of students attending private institutions for the state scholarship program

The California Master Plan for Higher Education, which is revised about every 10 years, is not a rigid blueprint to control centrally the development of California's system of higher education. Rather, it sets some general parameters; focuses primarily on the boundaries among the four sectors of higher education; and strives for a system that balances equity, quality, and efficiency.

Source: World Bank 1994.

To illustrate this point further, table 2.1 contrasts various types of tertiary education institutions by outlining the key factors that would combine to give each kind of institution the dimensions of excellence needed to be recognized as "world-class."

Even in the richest OECD countries, only a handful of institutions achieve the kind of concentration of top researchers, professors, students, facilities, and resources that world-class research universities enjoy as preconditions for excellence in scholarship. In the United States, for example, where more than 5,000 tertiary education institutions operate today, fewer than 30 universities are among the best in the world; in the United Kingdom, fewer than 10 universities; and in Japan, fewer than 5. Recent studies in the United States reveal a trend of increasing wealth concentration among the top universities, allowing them to invest sizable sums to expand their central role in research and offer luxurious facilities to attract top students and faculty.

Higher education is increasingly a tale of two worlds, with elite schools getting richer and buying up all the talent. It's only fitting that Whitman College, Princeton's new student residence, is named for eBay CEO Meg Whitman, because it's a billionaire's mansion in the form of a dorm. After Whitman (Class of '77) pledged $30 million, administrators tore up their budget and gave architect Demetri Porphyrios virtual carte blanche. Each student room has triple-glazed mahogany casement windows made of leaded

Table 2.1.   Defining Factors of Excellence for World-Class Tertiary Education Institutions

Type of institution	Concentration of talent	Abundance of resources	Favorable governance
Research university	Students and faculty Emphasis on graduate students	+++	+++
Teaching university/ college	Students and faculty Concentration on undergraduate students	++	+++
Community college	Diverse student body (academic achievement) Outstanding faculty with professional experience and pedagogical skills	+	+++
Open university	Diverse student body (academic achievement and age) Faculty with excellent skills for distance teaching	+	+++

Source: Created by Jamil Salmi.

glass. The dining hall boasts a 35-foot ceiling gabled in oak and a "state of the art servery." By the time the 10-building complex in the Collegiate Gothic style opened in August, it had cost Princeton $136 million, or $272,000 for each of the 500 undergraduates who will live there. Whitman College's extravagance epitomizes the fabulous prosperity of America's top tier of private universities.

BusinessWeek (2007)

The next relevant set of questions is about the most effective approach to achieve the proposed goal of becoming world-class. International experience shows that three basic strategies can be followed to establish world-class universities:

- Governments could consider upgrading a small number of existing universities that have the potential of excelling (picking winners).
- Governments could encourage a number of existing institutions to merge and transform into a new university that would achieve the type of synergies corresponding to a world-class institution (hybrid formula).
- Governments could create new world-class universities from scratch (clean-slate approach).

Each one of these approaches presents advantages and drawbacks that are now explored.

Upgrading Existing Institutions

One of the main benefits of this first approach is that the costs can be significantly less than those of building new institutions from scratch. This is the strategy followed by China since the early 1980s, with a sequence of carefully targeted reforms and investment programs (box 2.2). Indeed, Beijing University and Tsinghua University, China's top two universities, have been granted special privileges by the national authorities, allowing them to select the best students from every province before any other university, much to the consternation of the other leading universities around the country.

But this approach is unlikely to succeed in countries where the governance structure and arrangements that have historically prevented the emergence of world-class universities are not drastically revised. A comparison of the experiences of Malaysia and Singapore can serve to illustrate this point. Because Singapore was initially one of the provinces of the Malaysian Kingdom during the first few years following independence from the British, the contrasting stories of the University of Malaya and of the National University of Singapore (NUS) can be quite instructive, given their common cultural and colonial origins.

Box 2.2

Tertiary Education Reform in China

The Chinese government has been eager to develop a tertiary education system of international stature, and recent reform efforts reflect this goal. In 1993, the government adopted the *Guidelines of China's Educational Reform and Development*, which called for, among other things, building up 100 key universities with high-quality courses of specialized studies. In 1998, then-President Jiang Zemin announced the goal of building world-class universities, with a clear focus on the advancement of science and technology. Since then, state financing for tertiary education has more than doubled, reaching US$10.4 billion in 2003, or almost 1 percent of GDP. Several top universities received grants to improve institutional quality under the 985 Project, which reflects a conscious strategy to concentrate resources on a few institutions with the greatest potential for success at the international level.

Chinese universities are currently spending millions of dollars to recruit internationally renowned, foreign-trained Chinese and Chinese-American scholars and to build state-of-the-art research laboratories, particularly in science and technology. The strategy is to surround their star faculties with the brightest students, give them academic leeway, and provide competitive salaries and additional nonsalary incentives. With low labor costs, structural upgrades are achievable at a tenth of the cost of those in industrial countries. All this is happening in the context of a new regime of financial autonomy, significant cost sharing, and intense efforts to develop management expertise at all levels of university leadership.

Sources: French 2005; Mohrman 2003.

At independence, the University of Malaya operated as a two-campus university, one in Kuala Lumpur and the other in Singapore. The former evolved into the flagship University of Malaya from the very beginning, and the other became the University of Singapore, which merged with Nanyang University in 1980 to create NUS. By all global ranking measures, NUS today functions as a true world-class university (ranked 19th by the 2006 *THES*), while the University of Malaya struggles as a second-tier research university (ranked 192nd). In examining the different evolutionary paths of these two institutions, several factors appear to be constraining the University of Malaya's capacity to improve and innovate as effectively as NUS: affirmative action and restrictive admission policies, lower levels of financial support, and tightly controlled immigration regulations regarding foreign faculty.

The affirmative action policy implemented by the Malaysian government in favor of the children of the Malay majority population (*Bumiputras*) has significantly opened up opportunities for that segment of the population. The proportion of Malay students—the Malay population represents 52 percent of the total Malaysian population—went from about 30 percent to two-thirds of the total student population between the early 1970s and the late 1980s. The proportion of Chinese students decreased from 56 to 29 percent over the same period (Tierney and Sirat 2008).

The downside of these equity policies was that they prevented the university from being very selective in its student admissions to target the best and brightest in the country. Large numbers of academically qualified Chinese and Indian students, in particular, were unable to attend Malaysia's best universities and had to seek tertiary education abroad, thereby removing important talent from Malaysia.[1] In addition to restrictions among its own population, the Malaysian Ministry of Higher Education places a 5 percent cap on the number of foreign undergraduate students that public universities can enroll.

By contrast, the proportion of foreign students at NUS is 20 percent at the undergraduate level and 43 percent at the graduate level. The cost of their studies is highly subsidized by NUS. The primary consideration for attracting these foreign students is not to generate income, as often happens in U.K. and Australian universities, but to bring in highly qualified individuals who will enrich the pool of students.

NUS is also able to mobilize nearly twice as many financial resources as the University of Malaya (US$205 million annual budget versus US$118 million, respectively) through a combination of cost sharing, investment revenue, fund-raising, and government resources. The success of NUS's fund-raising efforts is largely the result of the generous matching-grant program set up by the government in the late 1990s as part of the Thinking Schools, Learning Nation Initiative, which provided a three-to-one matching at the beginning and is now down to one-to-one. As a result, the annual per student expenditures at NUS and the University of Malaya were US$6,300 and US$4,053, respectively, in 2006.

---

1 In the summer of 2008, for the first time in three decades of affirmative action policies, a Malay politician, the Chief Minister of the State of Selangor, dared question publicly the wisdom of continuing to apply the restrictive access rules toward the Chinese and Indian part of the population. His comments sparked off student demonstrations, encouraged by the vice-chancellor of the local university, and a rebuttal from the country's prime minister (Jardine 2008).

Finally, in Malaysia, on one hand, civil service regulations and a rigid financial framework make it difficult, if not impossible, to provide competitive compensation packages to attract the most competent professors and researchers, particularly foreign faculty. NUS, on the other hand, is not bound by similar legal constraints. The PS21 public service reform project in the early 2000s aimed at promoting a culture of excellence and innovation in all public institutions, including the two universities. NUS is therefore able to bring in top researchers and professors from all over the world, pay a global market rate for them, and provide performance incentives to stimulate competition and to retain the best and the brightest. Indeed, a good number of Malaysia's top researchers have been recruited by NUS.

Governments need, therefore, to construct a supportive external policy environment and create the financing and regulatory conditions that enable and encourage their universities to compete at an international level on a host of indicators on which the quality and relevance of university education are commonly assessed (see box 2.3), including reputation

---

Box 2.3

Do Governments Care about Higher Education? Lessons from the Soccer Field

For the sake of argument, let us consider the following: how would Barcelona's professional soccer team (FC Barcelona) perform if it were constrained by all the rules that burden our universities? What would happen if all the players were civil servants with salaries determined by a government ministry and if they were allowed to continue playing every day regardless of their performance during official games and behavior during practice sessions? What would happen if the club's income were not linked to its game results, if it could not pay higher salaries to attract the best players in the world, or if it could not quickly get rid of the underperforming players? What would happen if team strategy and tactics were decided by the government, rather than by the coach? Wouldn't such an approach risk relegating the Barcelona team to the sidelines of mediocrity? If we agree that such an approach is unwise for a sports team, why do we allow our universities to operate under such conditions? This suggests that, deep down, we care more about soccer than about the education of our children.

Source: Adapted by Jamil Salmi and Richard Hopper from Xavier Sala-i-Martín, "A Great Sense of Humor," *Vanguardia* (November 17, 2006). (Professor Sala-i-Martín teaches at Columbia University in the United States and Universidad Pompeu Fabra in Spain.)

and awards, foreign students and faculty, and research grants. One way to facilitate this is to grant management autonomy to the universities. Another is to provide performance-based financing, and a third is to put in place favorable taxation systems that allow companies and philanthropists to make tax-free donations to universities. The United States and India provide good examples of this practice.

Merging Existing Institutions

The second possible approach to building up a world-class university consists of promoting mergers among existing institutions. France and Denmark are two countries that have diligently embarked on this path in recent years. In France, individual universities and *grandes écoles* are exploring the feasibility of merging on a regional basis. In Denmark, the government has set up an Innovation Fund that would reward, among other things, the combination of similar institutions. In China, too, a number of mergers have taken place to consolidate existing institutions. For example, Beijing Medical University merged with Beijing University in 2000; similarly, in Shanghai, Fudan University merged with a medical university, and Zhejiang University was created out of the merger of five universities. In 2004, in the United Kingdom, the Victoria University of Manchester (VUM) and the University of Manchester Institute of Science and Technology (UMIST) merged, creating the largest university in the United Kingdom, with the purposefully stated goal of being "top 25 by 2015" (http://www.manchester.ac.uk/research/about/strategy/). Also in the United Kingdom recently, Cardiff University and the South Wales School of Medicine have merged as a deliberate step to establish a world-class university in Wales. These mergers, in most cases between already strong institutions, have often the explicit or implicit goal of creating larger and more comprehensive research universities in clear response to the fact that international rankings compare the number of publications and faculty awards of institutions independently from the size of their student enrollment (Harman and Harman 2008).

The government of the Russian Federation is also relying on amalgamation as a key policy within its overall strategy of developing elite research universities. In 2007, two pilot federal universities were set up by merging existing institutions in Rostov-on-Don in southern Russia and in the Siberian city of Krasnoyarsk. The two new institutions will also receive additional funding to support efforts to allow them to recruit highly qualified researchers and equip state-of-the-art laboratories (Holdsworth 2008).

The great advantage of mergers is that they can result in stronger institutions able to capitalize on the new synergies that their combined human and financial resources may generate. But mergers can also be risky, potentially aggravating problems instead of resolving them. In the case of France, for example, mergers would augment the critical mass of researchers and bring about a higher place in the SJTU ranking that favors research output, but they would not address the fundamental limitations of French universities, including inflexible admission policies, a weak financial basis, rigid governance arrangements, and outdated management practices. The Danish case, however, has greater chances of success because the push for mergers is taking place within the context of an overall governance reform aimed at transforming all universities in the country into more flexible and dynamic institutions (see appendix E).

Another danger associated with mergers is that the newly consolidated institution could suffer because of clashing institutional cultures. It has become clear, for example, that the previously mentioned merger between VUM and UMIST has not been as successful as expected or originally perceived. Currently acknowledging a £30 million budget deficit and the likelihood of up to 400 jobs lost on the campus, the University of Manchester has had immediate experience with the complexities of merging (Qureshi 2007). Among the main problems encountered are duplication of staff and curricular offerings, the political challenges of engendering support for the merger by making promises that have proven detrimental to keep (for example, committing to no compulsory redundancy at the time of merger and at present foreseeing a need to cut positions as rapidly as possible), and the short-term absorption of labor contracts and institutional debt. In addition, the newly formed institution, with its commitment to achieving world-class status, invested heavily in hiring "superstar" academic staff and supplying them with correspondingly superstar facilities. This exacerbated further the staffing debt that the institution inherited with the merging of the distinct and separate institutional staffs—and their individual cultures, norms, and labor contracts—into the one university. It remains to be seen how Manchester will address these financial, cultural, and interpersonal obstacles while simultaneously maintaining its quest for world-class status.

Thus, one of the main challenges when undertaking a merger is to create a shared academic culture and transformation vision among all constituting units (faculties, schools, departments) and bring internal coherence to the newly established institution. In many cases, the leaders of merged universities are severely constrained by the high level of independence claimed by constituting units. The new university established by merging existing universities may carry the legacy of the old brands, which in some cases may actually be an obstacle in attracting excellent students and staff. The leadership of the new, consolidated institution requires the political savvy to manage the various needs of conflicting constituents.

Creating New Institutions

In countries where institutional habits, cumbersome governance structures, and bureaucratic management practices prevent traditional universities from being innovative, creating new institutions may be the best approach, provided that it is possible to staff them with people not influenced by the culture of traditional universities and provided that financial resources are not a constraint. New institutions can emerge from the private sector, or governments can allow new public institutions to operate under a more favorable regulatory framework. Kazakhstan is a country intent on following this path as it seeks to make its economy less dependent on oil and more competitive overall. The government of Kazakhstan has decided to set up a new international university in Astana. The plan is that this university will follow a highly innovative multidisciplinary curriculum in cooperation with leading international universities. In the same vein, the government of Saudi Arabia announced in late 2007 its plans for a US$3 billion graduate research university, King Abdullah University of Science and Technology, which would operate outside the purview of the Ministry of Higher Education to allow for greater management autonomy and academic freedom than the regular universities of the kingdom enjoy.

One of the earlier success stories in that respect was the establishment of the Indian Institutes of Technology, which, in the past decades, have gradually risen to world-class status (box 2.4).

A third promising example is the creation of the Paris School of Economics (PSE) in February 2007, modeled after the London School of Economics and Political Science (LSE). This initiative combines elements of mergers with the creation of a brand new type of institution in the French context (Kahn and Malingre 2007). Cosponsored by four *grandes écoles*, the University of Paris I (the Sorbonne), and CNRS, PSE will operate as a private foundation regrouping the best economics departments from the participating institutions. Its initial funding comes not only from the state and the region but also from private companies and a U.S. foundation. Unlike traditional French universities, PSE will be highly selective in terms of incoming students. Many of the core professors will come from the most prestigious universities in the world.

Box 2.4

The Indian Institutes of Technology: A Success Story

Soon after becoming independent, India placed science and technology high on its economic development agenda. The first Indian Institute of Technology (IIT) was established in 1951 at Kharagpur (West Bengal), with support from the United Nations Educational, Scientific, and Cultural Organization (UNESCO), based on the MIT model. The second IIT was established at Bombay (now Mumbai) in 1958, with assistance from the Soviet Union through UNESCO. In 1959, IIT Madras (now Chennai) was established with assistance from Germany, and IIT Kanpur with help from a consortium of U.S. universities. British industry and the U.K. government supported the establishment of IIT Delhi in 1961. In 1994, IIT Guwahati was established totally through indigenous efforts. In 2001, the University of Roorkee was brought under the IIT family as the seventh such institution.

While taking advantage of experience and best practices in industrial countries, India ensured that the "institutions represented India's urges and India's future in making" (Prime Minister Nehru, 1956). The Indian Parliament designated them as "Institutes of National Importance," publicly funded institutions enjoying maximum academic and managerial freedom, offering programs of high quality and relevance in engineering, technology, applied sciences, and management at the undergraduate, master's, and doctorate levels and offering their own degrees. Student admissions are made strictly according to merit through a highly competitive common entrance test.

Today, the IITs attract the best students interested in a career in engineering and applied sciences. With 4,000 new students selected out of 250,000 applicants every year, the IITs are more selective than the top U.S. Ivy League schools. Several IIT alumni occupy the highest positions of responsibility in education, research, business, and innovation in several parts of the world. In 2005, *THES* ranked the collective IITs as, globally, the third-best engineering school after MIT and the University of California, Berkeley.

The main strength of the IITs has been their sustained ability to attract the best students and turn them into "creative engineers" or "engineer entrepreneurs." Initially, IITs were criticized for their contribution to the "brain drain" because about 40 percent of the graduates went abroad. Today, with the opening and fast growth of the Indian economy, this "weakness" is turning into a big strength for international cooperation and investments. Much of the success of Bangalore, for instance, is attributed to the phenomenon of "reverse brain drain."

Source: Created by Shashi Shrivastava and Jamil Salmi.

The creation of new institutions may also have the side benefit of stimulating existing ones into becoming more responsive to a more competitive environment. Examples from many parts of the world showing the emergence of high-quality private universities in countries with a predominantly public tertiary education sector have provoked the public universities into becoming more strategically focused. In Uruguay, the venerable University of the Republic—which had exercised a monopoly over tertiary education in the country for 150 years—started a strategic planning process and considered establishing postgraduate programs for the first time only after being confronted in the mid-1990s with competition from newly established private universities. Similarly, in Russia, the creation of the Higher School of Economics and of the Moscow School of Social and Economic Sciences in the 1990s pressured the Department of Economics at the State University of Moscow to revamp its curriculum and get more actively involved in international exchanges.

Maintaining the favorable conditions that are instrumental for the establishment of a new world-class institution requires constant vigilance, as the growing faculty shortage faced by the IITs illustrates. India's economic success has translated into a much larger income gap between the Institutes and industry than existed in the past. As a result, fewer promising graduates seek an academic career (Neelakantan 2007). It is estimated that the IITs are already suffering from a shortage of at least 900 qualified faculty. At the Delhi IIT alone, 29 percent of faculty positions are unfilled. Without the autonomy to raise salaries and offer more competitive employment packages, the IITs are at risk of losing their competitive edge. The younger Indian Institutes of Management face the same hurdle in their quest for world-class status (Bradshaw 2007).

The IITs and the Institutes of Management are also concerned about the recent decision of the Federal Ministry of Human Resource Development requiring them to implement a 49.5 percent quota ("reserved places") for various minority groups (Scheduled Castes, Scheduled Tribes, and Other Backward Classes) in the faculty. The institutions are asking the government to grant them the same exemption from reservation as the one given to the Tata Institute of Fundamental Research, the Bhabha Atomic Research Centre, and the Harish-Chandra Research Institute because of their status as "institutes of national importance" (Gupta 2008).

Finally, one of the major risks with implementing this third strategy in developing countries is that emulation by other institutions in the national tertiary education system may not be possible if most of the scarce public funds are concentrated in a few universities. Similarly, the good practices applied in the new institution(s) could simply not be applicable within the tight governance environment that usually binds public tertiary education institutions. This could lead to a highly dual system beyond what would be generally expected from a reasonably tiered system.

Evaluating these Approaches

Table 2.2 attempts to summarize the positive and negative aspects linked to each approach (upgrading, merging, or creating new institutions). It should be noted that these generic approaches are not mutually incompatible and that countries may pursue a combination of strategies based on these models.

Countries deciding to establish world-class universities by upgrading or merging existing ones must also choose an appropriate methodology

Table 2.2.   Costs and Benefits of Strategic Approaches for Establishing World-Class Universities

	Approach		
Conditions	Upgrading existing institutions	Merging existing institutions	Creating new institutions
Ability to attract talent	Difficult to renew staff and change the brand to attract top students	Opportunity to change the leadership and to attract new staff; existing staff may resist	Opportunity to select the best (staff and students); difficulties in recruiting top students to "unknown" institution; need to build up research and teaching traditions
Costs	Less expensive	Neutral	More expensive
Governance	Difficult to change mode of operation within same regulatory framework	More likely to work with legal status different from that of existing institutions	Opportunity to create appropriate regulatory and incentives framework
Institutional culture	Difficult to transform from within	May be difficult to create a new identity out of distinct institutional cultures	Opportunity to create culture of excellence
Change management	Major consultation and communication campaign with all stakeholders	"Normative" approach to educate all stakeholders about expected norms and institutional culture	"Environmentally adaptive" approach to communicate and socially market the new institution

Source: Created by Jamil Salmi.

to select which existing universities to merge. Governments need to assess the degree to which they want to manage the process in a centralized way, cherry-picking institutions where centers of excellence could be established or boosted, or whether it would be preferable to steer the tertiary education system at a distance, relying on broad strategic orientations and financial incentives to entice the most dynamic universities to transform themselves.

International experience suggests that in medium to large countries, the latter approach, which encourages competitive behaviors among tertiary education institutions, could be more effective in the long run. The China 211 and 985 projects, the Brain 21 program in South Korea, the German Initiative for Excellence, and the Millennium Institutes recently established in Chile are examples of how countries stimulate the creation or consolidation of research centers of excellence (box 2.5). Appendix F describes the most recent excellence initiatives implemented throughout the world.

Box 2.5

The German Initiative for Excellence

In January 2004, the German Federal Ministry of Education and Research launched a national competition to identify about 10 universities with the potential of becoming elite universities. Extra funding will be provided under three windows: to entire institutions aiming to become world-class universities, to centers of excellence with international recognition, and to graduate schools intent on strengthening the quality of their programs.

After initial resistance from the states jealous of their traditional authority in the area of tertiary education funding, a compromise was reached, and a joint commission was established, with representatives of the German Research Foundation and the Science Council.

In January 2006, the commission selected 10 universities among 27 candidates, 41 proposals for centers of excellence among 157 submissions, and 39 graduate schools among 135 proposals. The majority of selected universities (7 out of 10) are located in two states (Baden-Württemberg and Bavaria), and only 10 percent of the winning centers of excellence are in the humanities and social sciences. Most of the selected graduate schools have a strong multidisciplinary focus. A total of $2.3 billion of additional funding will be made available to support the winning proposals over a period of four years.

Source: Kehm 2006.

In smaller states, where the capacity for mobilizing and combining public and private resources is constrained, greater selectivity in investment funding may be a more appropriate approach to optimizing the deployment and utilization of public resources. In New Zealand, for instance, the country's premier tertiary education institution, the University of Auckland, has been calling for targeted government efforts to help transform the university into a leading research university:

> The Government's acknowledgement (through the reforms) that not all institutions are, or should be, the same is a critical and ultimately enabling first step towards the positioning of one or more New Zealand research universities as institutions of international quality and status. . . .
>
> The challenge New Zealand must address is that the most successful tertiary institutions in the world, those against which our best universities ought to be benchmarking themselves, operate with levels of public investment that we in New Zealand struggle to comprehend. To cite just one example, federal and state funding in the United States public universities is estimated at US\$12,000 per student – approximately twice that of New Zealand in equivalent purchasing terms. And that doesn't take into account the additional impact of the substantial endowments that many US universities enjoy. . . .
>
> A critical mass of leading staff and outstanding students in a university, enabled by adequate investment and an international reputation for teaching and research, produces research outputs, an atmosphere of intellectual excitement, and productive relationships with industry that cannot be replicated elsewhere. To cite just one example of what is possible, a November 2006 study by the Ministry of Research, Science and Technology found that of 16 New Zealand-developed drugs currently in clinical trials approved by the US Food and Drug Administration, 13 had been developed by our universities – and 12 of them by The University of Auckland!
>
> To reach this goal, and achieve the characteristics shared by world-class research universities, vision, commitment, and a desire for change are required. These will assist New Zealand's leading universities to provide a learning environment of the highest quality, to lead the advancement of knowledge creation, intellectual discovery, and innovation within New Zealand, and to take our place with world-class research universities on the global stage.
>
> Vision, commitment, and a desire for change will, however, not be sufficient. Increased levels of public and private investment will also be required, along with a particular commitment to the stated aim of the current reforms – differentiation. Both Australia and the US concentrate research excellence (and investment) in those institutions most likely to produce results for economic

and social development. We need the same willingness in New Zealand to recognize and fund excellence in a selective and strategic fashion. Only then will the current tertiary reforms be successful.

University of Auckland (2007)

The Role of Other Actors

It is important to stress that national governments are not the only major player when it comes to facilitating the establishment of world-class institutions. In large countries and federal systems, regional or provincial authorities often play a critical role, as illustrated by the active role played by the Californian authorities in designing and establishing an integrated system of tertiary education in the 1960s or more recently in establishing special Innovation Funds to strengthen linkages between the research universities and the regional economy. Similarly, in the past 10 years, the Shanghai municipality has given active support to its leading universities, especially Fudan University, as part of its accelerated development policies. In the State of Nuevo Leon in Mexico, the business community has also contributed substantially to the success of the Instituto Tecnológico y de Estudios Superiores de Monterrey (the Monterrey Institute of Technology and Higher Education, or ITESM).

The complementary role of the private sector in supporting the development of world-class universities should not be overlooked either. Private industry can make important financial contributions to help increase the endowment of top institutions, as happened in Singapore and Hong Kong, China. In some cases, philanthropists have even taken the initiative to launch a new institution with aspirations of excellence, as demonstrated by the examples of Olin College of Engineering in Massachusetts or Quest University Canada in British Columbia. An Indian billionaire, Anil Agarwal, gave US$1 billion to establish a multi-disciplinary research institution in Orissa, India. In Germany, Klaus Jacobs donated 200 million euros (€200 million) to the new private International University Bremen.

Besides potential funding, the active participation of private sector leaders on the board of the new institution(s) is important to steer its development. The contribution of the private sector can also take the form of close linkages to ensure inputs into the choice of relevant programs, the design of appropriate curricula, and full alignment of the new institution's applied research agenda with the needs of the local economy.

Strategic Dimensions at the Institutional Level

The first and perhaps most important aspect at this level is the quality of leadership and the strategic vision developed by the would-be world-class university. The second element is the proper sequencing of plans and activities envisaged to reach the proposed goal. Finally, particular attention needs to be given to the internationalization strategy of the university.

Leadership and Strategic Vision

The establishment of a world-class university requires, above all, strong leadership, a bold vision of the institution's mission and goals, and a clearly articulated strategic plan to translate the vision into concrete programs and targets. Figure 2.1 attempts to contrast the dynamics of a university that is on a renewal path with the stagnation path followed by institutions unwilling or unable to challenge themselves and their performance. Universities that aspire to better results engage in an objective assessment of their strengths and areas for improvement, set new stretch goals, and design and implement a renewal plan that can lead to improved performance. By contrast, as illustrated by the earlier discussion of the University of São Paulo, many institutions are complacent in their outlook, lack an ambitious vision of a better future, and continue to operate as they have in the past, ending up with a growing performance gap compared with that of their national or international competitors.

Recent research on university leadership suggests that in the case of top research universities, the best-performing institutions have leaders who combine good managerial skills and a successful research career (Goodall 2006). To be able to develop an appropriate vision for the future of the university and to implement this vision in an effective manner, the university president, vice-chancellor, or rector needs to fully understand the core agenda of the institution and to be able to apply the vision with the necessary operational skills.

A case study of the University of Leeds in the United Kingdom illustrates how the arrival of a new leader in 2003 marked the beginning of a conscious effort to reverse a downward trend through carefully planned and implemented strategic change. Rapid growth in student numbers (the second-largest university in the United Kingdom) had led to tensions between the teaching and research missions of the university, resulting in diminishing research income and results. Among the main challenges faced by the new vice-chancellor was the need to create a sense of urgency among the entire university community and to convince everyone of the importance of achieving a better alignment between corporate

Figure 2.1.   The Stagnation and Change Diamonds

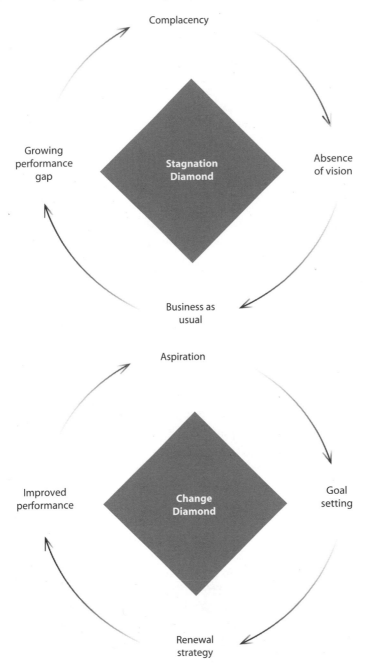

Source: Adapted from Perry and Sherlock (2008).

goals and the contribution of individual faculties and departments with a long tradition of autonomy.

> For the University of Leeds, our reputation and profile made this challenge harder. As a great institution we had to demonstrate the vulnerability of our current position, alongside the importance and achievability of our vision. Staff were not going to engage in a strategy unless its credibility and relevance could be clearly established. To achieve this we used a variety of internal and external measures of performance reputation and ranking to clearly articulate the current position and the vision. . . . Considerable time and effort was dedicated to developing the vision of "by 2015 our distinctive ability to integrate world-class research, scholarship and education will have secured us a place among the top 50 universities in the world."
>
> Donoghue and Kennerley (forthcoming)

A crucial element of the vision is the selection of a niche market toward which the institution will seek to build and maximize its comparative advantage. In that respect, it is important to underline that a university—even a world-class university—most likely cannot excel in all areas. Harvard University, widely recognized as the number one institution of higher learning in the world, is not the best-ranked university in all disciplines (see examples in table 2.3). Its strengths are especially noted in economics, medical sciences, education, political science, law, business studies, English, and history.

Part of the vision setting will therefore consist of delineating the main areas where the institution wishes and has the potential to operate at the forefront. Some world-class institutions, such as the Indian Institutes of Technology, have specialized in a few engineering disciplines. The London School of Economics and Political Science is best known for outstanding scholarship in economics, sociology, political science, and anthropology. Even though no Swiss university appears among the top 50 internationally, the Ecole hôtelière de Lausanne (the Lausanne Hotel School), the only European school accredited by the New England Association of Schools and Colleges, is considered to be among the best in the world, on par with the University of Nevada's College of Hotel Administration and Cornell University's School of Hotel Administration.

Institutions aspiring to become world-class universities do not need to replicate what the current top universities do; they can innovate in many different ways. One possible path is to adopt a radically different approach to organizing the curriculum and pedagogy of the institution, as the newly established Olin College of Engineering in Massachusetts in the United

Table 2.3.   Rankings by Discipline in _U.S. News & World Report_, 2008

Rank	Business	Criminology	Education	Engineering	Law	Medicine
1	Harvard University	University of Maryland, College Park	Stanford University	MIT	Yale University	Harvard University
2	Massachusetts Institute of Technology (MIT)	Rutgers, the State University of New Jersey	Teachers College, Columbia University	Georgia Institute of Technology	Columbia University	University of Pennsylvania
3	Northwestern University	University of California, Irvine	University of Oregon	University of Illinois at Urbana-Champaign	New York University	University of California, San Francisco
4	Stanford University	State University of New York (SUNY) at Albany	Vanderbilt University	Stanford University	Harvard University	Johns Hopkins University
5	University of Pennsylvania	University of Cincinnati	University of California, Los Angeles (UCLA)	University of California, Berkeley	Stanford University	Washington University in St. Louis

Source: U.S. News & Report 2008.

States and the Limkokwing University of Creative Technology in Malaysia have attempted in the field of engineering and technology.

The Franklin W. Olin College of Engineering was founded in 1999 with a US$400 million endowment from the Olin Foundation and the mandate to implement an innovative engineering curriculum. Olin College seeks to produce graduates trained in the new skills identified in a 2005 report, *Educating the Engineer of 2020*, such as competency in teamwork, communication, entrepreneurial thinking, creativity and design, and cross-disciplinary thinking (NAE 2005). Most of the learning at Olin takes place through design-build team projects. All students are required to complete a program in the fundamentals of business and entrepreneurship, as well as a special project in the arts, humanities, or social sciences. To foster its philosophy of interdisciplinary work, the college does not have any academic departments. To encourage a culture of continuous innovation and risk taking among professors, there is also no tenure system at Olin. All students receive merit scholarships to cover the cost of tuition and living expenses in Olin's residential environment (Miller 2007a).

Even though it is too early to draw definitive conclusions—the first batch of graduates completed their degrees in May 2006—there are clear indications that the Olin College of Engineering has managed to attract talented students and excellent faculty, to put in place an innovative and stimulating curriculum, and to develop a culture of intellectual empowerment. Its graduates appear to be successful in finding appealing jobs or accessing top graduate schools (Schwartz 2007).

Similarly, the Limkokwing University of Creative Technology in Malaysia has established itself as an innovative private institution emphasizing the acquisition of creativity and design competencies relevant to a wide array of activities in industry and services. The rapid development of its new campuses in Botswana, Lesotho, and London attests to the success of its model.

Another innovative approach links the transformation of the institution to shifting regional or local development opportunities, as illustrated by the example of Clemson University in South Carolina, United States (see box 2.6).

Sometimes, going through a crisis can energize an institution into changing its culture and revitalizing itself, as happened with the Catholic University of Leuven (Belgium) in the late 1960s after it faced a large financial deficit (Hatakenaka 2007). Today, it ranks among the top European universities.

Box 2.6

Developing a New Vision at Clemson University

Clemson University, a land-grant university in South Carolina traditionally focused on agriculture and mechanical engineering, has undertaken a radical transformation process in recent years. Based on an in-depth analysis of the conversion of South Carolina into one of the leading automotive regions in the United States, Clemson University formed a strategic partnership with the German automaker BMW with the aim of re-creating itself as the premier automotive and motor sports research and education university. Its new vision statement specifically mentions the target of becoming one of the nation"s top 20 public universities (as measured by *U.S. News & World Report*), up from the rank of 74th four years ago and 34th in 2005

Source: Presentation by Chris Przirembel, Vice-President for Research and Economic Development, Clemson University, at the MIT Conference on Local Innovation Systems, Cambridge, MA, December 13, 2005.

The Pontifical Catholic University of Peru (in Lima) went through a similar positive transformation in the late 1990s after a drastic reduction in student enrollment that led the university to undertake a thorough strategic planning exercise. Concerned that student demand was diminishing because of the location of the university in an area of the capital city that had lost its appeal over the years, the leadership thought briefly about moving to a new site, close to where the middle classes were now living. But extensive consultations with stakeholders during the strategic planning period made the university aware that the fundamental issue was one of deteriorating quality and relevance. Drastic renewal measures were taken, including course redesign and a strong emphasis on continuous quality monitoring and improvement, resulting in higher student demand and successful fund-raising.[2]

It is finally important to underline that the efforts of universities seeking to transform themselves should be really of a strategic nature, based on a forward-looking vision that is genuinely innovative. With the growing influence of rankings documented at the beginning of this report, institutions should resist the temptation to focus on limited actions that are directly related to the specific indicators used by the rankers and not necessarily linked to a change vision. There is a risk, for

---

2 Based on a series of visits and interviews by the author between 1998 and 2001.

example, in paying too much attention to factors such as admission scores and donations from alumni that receive prominence in many national rankings to the detriment of other key aspects that may be more important from an educational viewpoint. The research productivity emphasis of the main two world rankings contributes also to reinforcing this research drift trend and results in skewed reward systems that favor research productivity over the quality of teaching and learning. Mergers of convenience, driven mainly by size concerns, are another illustration of this kind of misguided behavior.

> The subjective nature of world class status means that institutions will attempt to address those dimensions that are considered in assessing reputations and that are visible. In this respect, research activity, publications, citations, and major faculty awards are highly visible and measurable while the quality of the educational process is not. Thus, it is not surprising to see a focus on research criteria in the surveys and in the efforts of institutions to promote their importance and little or no attempt to measure and assess teaching quality or educational activities. Indeed, there is a tacit assumption that if an institution is highly competitive in its admissions that the educational quality is also very high, even without measuring that quality. Yet, student competition for admission may be based upon a prestigious reputation that is largely due to the research visibility of a university rather than its educational virtues.
>
> Levin, Jeong, and Ou (2006)

Sequencing

Time is an important dimension that also needs to be factored into the strategic plan of the aspiring world-class university. Developing a culture of excellence does not happen from one day to the next. Proper sequencing of interventions and careful balance among the various quantitative objectives are required to avoid experiencing the kinds of growing pains that some of the Chinese universities have encountered (box 2.7).

It is important to stress that vision development and strategic planning are not one-time exercises. In a highly competitive environment, the more successful organizations in both business and academia are those that are relentless in challenging themselves in the pursuit of better and more effective ways of responding to client needs. With constant replenishment of intellectual capital, performance is never static in the best universities. The most successful institutions are not content with relying on past accomplishments, but always aspire to be among the best in the world. They are successful in creating, internally, a supportive atmosphere that encourages everyone to define and pursue stretch goals.

Box 2.7

Obstacles to the Transformation of Chinese Universities

There are signs that China's plans to achieve world-class stature are meeting some obstacles. First is the concern that Chinese universities have expanded too quickly at the expense of maintaining quality. Second, the academic culture that demands quick results hampers innovative and long-term research efforts. While the "publish or perish" culture is strong in the United States, such pressures are often balanced with the recognition of the value of creativity and originality. Lack of undergraduate students with a strong foundation in science and technology is the third weakness. Without well-trained students entering the graduate programs, first-class faculty and laboratories will be underutilized. Fourth, lack of academic freedom is a serious issue in China. Faculty and students are encouraged to question government policies or engage in debates on pressing issues in only a limited way, with some disincentive for creative thinking.

Finally, China's vision of world-class universities focuses almost exclusively on factors such as increased publications in international journals, up-to-date laboratories, more buildings, star professors, and additional funding (Mohrman 2003). Yet the vision is largely imitative, rather than creative. Ruth Simmons (2003), president of Brown University, emphasizes the importance of other factors: "The bedrock of university quality in the United States is peer review, a system in which standards are set by leaders of the field and those leaders are themselves challenged and judged by this process." Simmons goes on to note that "universities promote the capacity of scholars to develop original work that is not immediately applicable or useful. Great universities are not only useful in their own time, but in preparing for future times. What allows a great university to do that is as little interference from the state as possible. The role of the state is to provide resources, but to give wide latitude to universities' leaders to decide how scholarship is to advance." Their universities might do better to focus on building world-class departments, institutes, or schools, rather than trying to excel on all accounts.

Source: Altbach 2003.

This is one of the characteristics of the Olin College of Engineering, whose president defined the challenge of continuous improvement in the following terms:

Innovation and continuous improvement require certain cultural attitudes and commitments. First, an implicit humility is required to embrace the notion that improvement is always possible, and that we can always learn from others outside our community. Listening to those outside academia has not always been the strong suit of American higher education. In addition, continuous improvement is only possible if continuous assessment is employed to guide the process. We must be willing to expose ourselves to review and measurement, and to take the time to learn from our mistakes. Finally and perhaps most importantly, continuous improvement requires openness to change.

Miller (2007b)

Not even the most famous universities are immune from the necessity of evolving and adapting to changing circumstances, as the University of Oxford's failed attempt at financial reform illustrates. In the current increasingly competitive market for academics, central authorities at the university face the need for additional resources to continue hiring internationally renowned professors and researchers. They have been constrained, however, by centuries-old governance arrangements and authority structures that give the control of a large share of the university's wealth to its individual colleges. The colleges have no desire to share their resources coming from traditional endowments and a large intake of foreign postgraduate students whose fees are more than three times higher than those paid by domestic students.

One aspect of the reform proposals submitted in 2006 by Vice-Chancellor John Hood, who had been recruited from New Zealand to lead Oxford in attempting to redress the balance, was to give more power over these resources to the university's central leadership, while also allowing for increased financial oversight by outsiders. The reform was ultimately rejected by Oxford's academic community, leading to Hood's decision to step down at the end of his five-year term in 2009. A number of alumni have expressed concern about the potentially negative consequences of these arrangements, which may have resulted in academic overload and lack of proper supervision of postgraduate students (Shultziner 2008).

Internationalization Dimension

One way of accelerating the transformation into a world-class university is to use internationalization strategies effectively. An influx of top foreign students can be instrumental in upgrading the academic level of the student population and enriching the quality of the learning experience through the multicultural dimension. In this regard, the capacity to offer programs in a foreign language, especially English, can be a powerful attraction factor. Among the 100 top universities according to the SJTU ranking, 11 come from non-native-English-speaking countries where some graduate programs are offered in English (Denmark, Finland, Israel, the Netherlands, Norway, Sweden, and Switzerland).

As discussed earlier, the ability to attract foreign professors and researchers is also an important determinant or characteristic of excellence. Universities need to be able to offer incentives, including flexible remuneration and employment conditions, to recruit top academics from other countries. These talented individuals can help upgrade existing departments or establish graduate programs and research centers in new areas of competitive advantage. In the United Kingdom, for example, 27 percent of all academic staff appointed in 2005/06 were foreign nationals (Universities UK 2007). In cases in which it is difficult to attract foreign faculty on a full-time basis, the university can start by bringing in leading foreign scholars on a temporary basis.

To facilitate the contribution of foreign scholars, a number of aspiring world-class universities have formed fruitful partnerships with top universities in industrial countries. This was the case with the Indian Institutes of Technology in the early years of their establishment (see box 2.4). More recently, one emerging world-class university, the National University of Singapore, has relied extensively on strategic alliances with the Australian National University, Duke University, Eindhoven University of Technology in the Netherlands, Harvard University, Johns Hopkins University, MIT, and Tsinghua University in China, to mention only the better-known partner institutions. These partnerships have not always functioned smoothly, however, as shown by the recent rupture with Johns Hopkins University in Singapore because of dissatisfaction with the quality of faculty and outputs offered by the foreign partner (Normile 2006).

Attracting leading scholars from the diaspora is another internationalization strategy that a few universities in India and China have implemented with success (Brown 2007). Beijing University, for example, has hired hundreds of academics of Chinese origin. As part of its human resource strategy, the university closely monitors good Chinese scholars abroad and creates favorable conditions for their return. Mexico, Scotland, and South Africa have also started to implement interesting strategies to harness the contribution of talented nationals living outside the country (see box 2.8).

Related to this internationalization dimension of improving an institution's global reputation is the extent to which national researchers

Box 2.8

How Diasporas Can Contribute to Development in Home Countries

A diaspora is a network of people coming from a same home country and living abroad. A successful diaspora network is characterized by the following three elements: (a) members of the diaspora are talented and show strong intrinsic motivation; (b) they are involved in project implementation in their home country and serve as connectors, catalysts, or vectors for projects development in the home country; (c) its efficiency, continuity, and development over time are based on concrete activities with measurable outcomes.

In most cases, diasporas and expatriate networks emerge spontaneously. Government interventions can help develop or structure such initiatives, however. The first condition required for home countries to take advantage of these expatriate talents is to recognize them as an opportunity to develop a knowledge-based economy. Strategies to leverage diasporas vary with the country conditions on one hand and the diaspora's characteristics on the other hand. Nevertheless, a common and critical element to efficiently use expatriate talent is the existence of solid institutions.

An excellent illustration of an efficient diaspora search network is GlobalScot, a network of high-powered Scots from all over the world who use their expertise and influence as antennae, bridges, and springboards to generate projects in Scotland. Launched in 2002, this network has proven extremely attractive and efficient, with 850 influential businesspeople participating in 2005, and therefore contributing to Scotland's economic development strategy. ChileGlobal, Mexico's Network of Talent Abroad, and the Global South Africans project have inspired themselves from the GlobalScot model and are on their way to successfully adapting it to their respective specificities.

Diasporas as search networks can be compared with, and learn from, alumni networks. There is a great opportunity for tertiary institutions to participate in the diaspora network process. Universities have a potent comparative advantage to follow distinctive alumni, identify leaders abroad, and gradually build a search network. This is how successful diasporas begin.

Source: Kuznetsov 2006.

have the linguistic competence to publish in English. One way in which institutions and academics advance their reputation is by their presence in scientific publications. Because citation indexes compile data primarily from journals published in English, the facility with which academics can disseminate research results in English becomes a critical factor in enhancing institutional reputation. Needless to say, institutions functioning in English are more likely to engender such success.

In some cases, universities have also found it useful to hire a foreign professional to lead the institution through the proposed transformation process. Australia, the Republic of Korea, and the United Kingdom are examples of countries where this has happened in recent years. Of course, this approach is not always welcome. Bringing in an outsider to lead a flagship university can hurt national sensitivities, and few countries have shown the disposition to undertake international recruitment searches to fill the highest university positions. Regardless, this is one way in which institutions can challenge themselves into "thinking outside the box" and embrace a change management mind-set.

It is also important to remember that those institutions that are deemed to be the most world-class are also thinking outside the box and perpetually seeking ways to sustain their top positions. As students seek excellence in higher education, regardless of borders, the best universities in the world must change how they compete to attract these students to their campuses (box 2.9).

Box 2.9

When "the Best" Compete for You: China's Rise

Much is made of the cultural drive that brings Chinese students to the U.S., U.K., and other world-renowned higher education systems. What has received somewhat less attention is the development of the Chinese higher education system into one that challenges the supremacy of the historically powerful Western institutions. This rise in local quality has generated a global competition to attract the best students to faraway campuses.

Eager to cultivate generations of students in this new frontier, admissions officers from premier American universities are scouring China to recruit top high school students who may dismiss such colleges as out of reach and unaffordable. In last month's campaign during the contest, representatives of Harvard, Brown, and Stanford Universities touted liberal arts education, research opportunities, and American dorm life to students and their parents, even promising full scholarships.

(continued)

> **Box 2.9** *(continued)*
>
> "There are no quotas, no limits on the number of Chinese students we might take," Fitzsimmons told a standing-room-only crowd of more than 300 students during a visit to Beijing No. 4 High School. "We know there are very good students from China not applying now. I hope to get them into the pool to compete."
>
> That message is disconcerting for American students toiling to land a coveted spot in Harvard's 1,660-student freshman class and controversial among some educators. But Fitzsimmons and others say that they had better get used to the idea: "Applications from China have exploded in recent years as the Communist country opens up to the world, and they're only going to increase."
>
> *Source:* Jan 2008.

Attracting the best—students, scholars, and research partners—from anywhere they can be found has become the modus operandi of the world's best institutions. As borders become softer, the competition for the best has become more intense.

In the case of science-and-technology–oriented universities, the ability to attract research contracts from foreign firms and multinational corporations is a good measure of the scientific standing of rising universities. In recent years, a few Chinese and Indian universities have received important research contracts from North American and European firms, sometimes at the expense of universities in the countries of origin of these companies (Yusuf and Nabeshima 2007).

Summary Checklist

The following critical questions need to be answered to guide the quest toward establishing world-class universities:

At the National Level

- Why does the country need a world-class university? What are the economic rationale and the expected added value compared with the contribution of existing institutions?
- What is the vision for this university? What niche will it occupy?
- What would be the investment and recurrent costs of a world-class university?
- How many world-class universities are desirable and affordable as a public sector investment?

- What strategy would work best in the country context: upgrading existing institutions, merging existing institutions, or creating new institutions?
- What should be the selection process among existing institutions if the first or second approach is chosen?
- What will be the relationship and articulation between the new institution(s) and existing tertiary education institutions?
- How will the transformation be financed? What share should fall under the public budget? What share should be borne by the private sector? What incentives should be offered (for example, land grants and tax exemptions)?
- What are the governance arrangements that must be put in place to facilitate this transformation and support suitable management practices? What level of autonomy and forms of accountability will be appropriate?
- What will the government's role be in this process?

At the Institutional Level
- How can the institution build the best leadership team?
- What are the vision and mission statements, and what are the specific goals that the university is seeking to achieve?
- In what niche(s) will it pursue excellence in teaching and research?
- What is the target student population?
- Should the university be set up in partnership with a foreign institution? And what type of partnership should be sought?
- What are the internationalization goals that the university needs to achieve (with regard to faculty, students, programs, and so forth)?
- What is the likely cost of the proposed qualitative leap, and how is it going to be funded?
- How will success be measured? What monitoring systems, outcome indicators, and accountability mechanisms will be used?

Implications for the World Bank

In the tertiary education sector, the World Bank's work with governments in developing and transition countries has focused essentially on systemwide issues and reforms. World Bank assistance has combined policy advice, analytical work, capacity-building activities, and financial support through loans and credits to facilitate and accompany the design and implementation of major tertiary education reforms.

In recent years, however, a growing number of countries have asked the World Bank to help them identify the main obstacles preventing their universities from becoming world-class universities and map out ways of transforming them toward this goal. To accommodate these requests, the World Bank has found that it needs to consider how to align support for individual institutions with its traditional emphasis on systemwide innovations and reforms. Experiences to date suggest that this goal can be achieved through three types of complementary interventions that would be combined in a variety of configurations under different country circumstances:

- Technical assistance and guidance to assist countries in (a) identifying possible options and affordability; (b) deciding the number of elite universities that they need and can fund in a sustainable way, based on analysis guided by existing and projected financial constraints; (c) defining in each case the specific mission and niche of the institution; and (d) working out the articulation with the rest of the tertiary education system to avoid resource allocation distortions.

- Facilitation and brokering to help new elite institutions get exposure to relevant international experience through workshops and study tours. This can involve linking up with foreign partner institutions that can provide capacity-building support during the start-up years of the new institution or the transformation period of an existing institution aspiring to become world-class. The World Bank can also facilitate policy dialogue by bringing different stakeholders and partners together to agree on the vision and to garner support for the new institution(s).

- Financial support to fund preinvestment studies for the design of the project and investment costs for the actual establishment of the planned institution.

In countries that have established a positive regulatory and incentive framework to promote the development of private tertiary education, International Finance Corporation (IFC) loans and guarantees can also be used to complement or replace World Bank Group financial support if the target university or universities are set up or transformed as public–private partnerships.

It is, of course, important to tailor these options to specific country situations. Upper-middle-income countries are unlikely to be seeking financial aid as such, but are definitely looking for advice reflecting the World Bank's comparative advantage as both a knowledge broker and an observer of international experience. This advice could be provided on a fee-for-service basis.

Middle-income countries may be interested in receiving both technical and financial assistance. Based on the World Bank's experience with Innovation Funds in a large number of countries (Saint 2006), using a competitive approach could be envisaged to ensure that funding goes to those institutions that have formulated the most innovative strategic visions and developed well-thought-out implementation plans.

Low-income countries, especially those of relatively small size (fewer than 5 million inhabitants), confront a unique set of challenges in their efforts to establish a flagship institution that could address critical human skills requirements and advanced research needs. They can rarely marshal

Table 3.1.   Type of World Bank Support by Country Group

Type of assistance	Upper-middle-income	Middle-income	Low-income (large states)	Low-income (small states)
Technical assistance	Yes	Yes	Yes	Yes
Facilitation / brokering	Yes	Yes	Yes	Yes
Financial support	No	Yes (competitive basis)	Yes	Yes (regional)

Source: Created by Jamil Salmi.

sufficient resources to set up and sustain a high-cost institution and have a limited number of qualified faculty to provide training and conduct research at an internationally competitive level. In these cases, developing a regional institution could be more appropriate to achieve economies of scale and mobilize financial and human resources in a more cost-effective way. For capacity-building purposes, donor support for the development or strengthening of such programs should not be limited only to the initial capital outlay but must also include funding (on a declining basis) for long-term maintenance and incentives to attract and retain qualified professionals.

Table 3.1 summarizes the various forms of support that could be provided to help different categories of countries as they move to transform their universities into world-class universities or establish new flagship institutions from scratch.

Conclusion

> Good is the enemy of great.
>
> Jim Collins

The highest-ranked universities are the ones that make significant contributions to the advancement of knowledge through research, teach with the most innovative curricula and pedagogical methods under the most conducive circumstances, make research an integral component of undergraduate teaching, and produce graduates who stand out because of their success in intensely competitive arenas during their education and (more important) after graduation. It is these concrete accomplishments and the international reputation associated with these sustained achievements that make these institutions world-class.

There is no universal recipe or magic formula for "making" a world-class university. National contexts and institutional models vary widely. Therefore, each country must choose, from among the various possible pathways, a strategy that plays to its strengths and resources. International experience provides a few lessons regarding the key features of such universities—high concentrations of talent, abundance of resources, and flexible governance arrangements—and successful approaches to move in that direction, from upgrading or merging existing institutions to creating new institutions altogether.

Regardless of institutional commitment or capacity to improve, building a world-class university does not happen overnight. No matter how much money is thrown at the endeavor, instant results are impossible. Achieving the goals of creating a culture of excellence and achieving high-quality outputs take many years and sustained commitment on the part of the entire constituency of the institution, internal and external.

Furthermore, the transformation of the university system cannot take place in isolation. A long-term vision for creating world-class universities—and its implementation—should be closely articulated with (a) the country's overall economic and social development strategy, (b) ongoing changes and planned reforms at the lower levels of the education system, and (c) plans for the development of other types of tertiary education institutions to build an integrated system of teaching, research, and technology-oriented institutions.

It is important to note that although world-class institutions are commonly equated with top research universities, there are also world-class tertiary education institutions that are neither research focused nor operate as universities in the strictest interpretation of the term. The U.K. Open University, for example, is widely recognized as the premier distance education institution in the world, and yet it does not make the international rankings. Conestoga College in Ontario, Canada, is ranked as the best community college in Canada, and in Germany, the Fachhochschulen of Mannheim and Bremen have outstanding reputations. In the United States, a new ranking of community colleges, based on the quality of teaching and learning, seems to imply that the top institutions, at the least, outperform some of the best four-year universities in the country (Carey 2007). Two European countries that have achieved remarkable progress as emerging knowledge economies, Finland and Ireland, do not boast any university among the top 50 in the world, but they have excellent technology-focused institutions. International rankings clearly favor research-intensive universities at the cost of excluding first-rate institutions that primarily enroll undergraduate students. Liberal arts schools such as Wellesley, Carleton, Williams, and Pomona Colleges are all considered among the very best undergraduate teaching institutions in the United States.

As countries embark on the task of establishing world-class universities, they must also consider the need to create, besides research universities, excellent alternative institutions to meet the wide range of education and training needs that the tertiary education system is expected to satisfy. The growing debate on measuring learning outcomes at the tertiary education level, fueled by the recommendations of the 2005 Spellings Commission on the Future of Higher Education in the United States and OECD's 2008 initiative on Assessing Higher Education Learning Outcomes (AHELO) to study the feasibility of carrying out an international assessment of higher-education outcomes, is testimony to the recognition that excellence is not only about achieving outstanding results with outstanding students but ought perhaps to be also measured in terms of how much added value is given by institutions in addressing the specific learning needs of an increasingly diverse student population.

Finally, the building pressures and momentum behind the push for world-class universities must be examined within the proper context to avoid overdramatization of the value and importance of world-class institutions and distortions in resource allocation patterns within national tertiary education systems. Even in a global knowledge economy, where every nation, both industrial and developing, is seeking to increase its share of the economic pie, the hype surrounding world-class institutions far exceeds the need and capacity for many systems to benefit from such advanced education and research opportunities, at least in the short term. Indeed, in some countries where the existing tertiary education institutions are of higher quality than the economic opportunities available to graduates, excellent tertiary education may exacerbate existing brain-drain problems.

As with other service industries, not every nation needs comprehensive world-class universities, at least not while more fundamental tertiary education needs are not being met. World-class research institutions require huge financial commitments, a concentration of exceptional human capital, and governance policies that allow for top-notch teaching and research. Many nations would likely benefit from an initial focus on developing the best national universities possible, modeled perhaps on those developed as the land-grant institutions in the United States during the 19th century or the polytechnic universities of Germany and Canada. Such institutions would emphasize the diverse learning and training needs of the domestic student population and economy. Focusing efforts on the local community and economy, such institutions could lead to more effective and sustainable development than broader world-class aspirations. Regardless, institutions will inevitably, from here on out, be increasingly subject to comparisons and rankings, and those deemed to be the best in these rankings of research universities will continue be considered the very best in the world.

Comparison of the Methodologies for the Main International Rankings

Criteria	Webometrics		ARWU (Shanghai)		THES (Times)	
Universities analyzed	13000		2000		500+	
Universities ranked	4000		500		200	
Quality of education			Alumni Nobel and Fields Medal	10%	Student/staff ratio	20%
Internationalization					International students	5%
					International staff	5%
Size	Web size (2x)	25%	Size of institution	10%		
Research output	Rich Files (1x)	12.5%	*Nature & Science*	20%		
	Google Scholar (1X)	12.5%	SCI & SSCI	20%		
Prestige	Link visibility (4x)	50%	Staff Nobel and Fields Medal	20%	Academic peer review	40%
					Reputation: employers	10%
Impact			Highly cited researchers	20%	Citations	20%

Sources: Webometrics 2008; SJTU 2008; QS-Top Universities 2008.
Note: ARWU = Academic Ranking of World Universities.

Shanghai Jiao Tong University (SJTU) 2008 ARWU Country Ranking

Country/region ranking	Country/region	Rank of top university in country/region
1	United States	1
2	United Kingdom	4
3	Japan	19
4	Switzerland	24
4	Canada	24
6	France	42
7	Denmark	45
8	Netherlands	47
9	Sweden	51
10	Germany	55
11	Australia	59
12	Norway	64
13	Israel	65
14	Finland	68
15	Russian Federation	70
16–20	Belgium, Brazil, Italy, Singapore	101–51
21–26	Argentina; Austria; Republic of Korea; Mexico; Spain; Taiwan, China	152–200
27–33	China; Czech Republic; Greece; Hong Kong, China; Ireland; New Zealand; South Africa	201–302
34–36	Hungary, India, Poland	303–401
37–40	Chile, Portugal, Slovenia, Turkey	402–503

Source: SJTU 2008.

The Times Higher Education Supplement (THES) 2008 Country Ranking

Country/region ranking	Country/region	Rank of top university in country/region
1	United States	1
2	United Kingdom	2
3	Australia	16
4	Japan	19
5	Canada	20
6	Switzerland	24
7	Hong Kong, China	26
8	France	28
9	Singapore	30
10	Denmark	48
11	Ireland	49
12	China	50
13	Republic of Korea	50
14	Netherlands	53
15	Germany	57
16	Sweden	63
17	New Zealand	65
18	Belgium	72
19	Finland	91
20	Israel	93

(continued)

Country/region ranking	Country/region	Rank of top university in country/region
21	Austria	115
22	Taiwan, China	124
23	Mexico	150
24	India	154
25	Thailand	166
26	Norway	177
27	South Africa	179
28	Russian Federation	183
29	Spain	186
30	Italy	192
31	Brazil	196
32	Argentina	197
33	Greece	200

Source: THES 2008.

Key Characteristics of World-Class Universities

A world-class university

- Has an international reputation for its research;
- Has an international reputation for its teaching;
- Has a number of research stars and world leaders in their fields;
- Is recognized not only by other world-class universities (for example, U.S. Ivy League) but also outside the world of higher education;
- Has a number of world-class departments (that is, not necessarily all);
- Identifies and builds on its research strengths and has a distinctive reputation and focus (that is, its "lead" subjects);
- Generates innovative ideas and produces basic and applied research in abundance;
- Produces groundbreaking research output recognized by peers and prizes (for example, Nobel Prize winners);
- Attracts the most able students and produces the best graduates;
- Can attract and retain the best staff;
- Can recruit staff and students from an international market;
- Attracts a high proportion of postgraduate students, both taught and research;
- Attracts a high proportion of students from overseas;

- Operates within a global market and is international in many activities (for example, research links, student and staff exchanges, and throughput of visitors of international standing);
- Has a very sound financial base;
- Receives large endowment capital and income;
- Has diversified sources of income (for example, government, private companies sector, research income, and overseas student fees);
- Provides a high-quality and supportive research and educational environment for both its staff and its students (for example, high-quality buildings and facilities/high-quality campus);
- Has a first-class management team with strategic vision and implementation plans;
- Produces graduates who end up in positions of influence and/or power (that is, movers and shakers such as prime ministers and presidents);
- Often has a long history of superior achievement (for example, the Universities of Oxford and Cambridge in the United Kingdom and Harvard University in the United States);
- Makes a big contribution to society and our times;
- Continually benchmarks with top universities and departments worldwide; and
- Has the confidence to set its own agenda.

Source: Alden and Lin 2004.

Tertiary Education Reform in Denmark: The University Act of 2003

Through reforms in four key areas—institutional autonomy, institutional leadership, quality assurance, and internationalization—Denmark is in the process of transforming its university system into an independent sector contributing to broad national success by answering more effectively to the evolving labor market that it serves.

Institutional Autonomy: Increased Independence for Denmark's Universities

- As of 2003, all universities in Denmark are considered independent subsidiaries of the Ministry of Science, Technology, and Innovation.
- Funds are distributed based on established rates for research and on per student enrollments and completion, to establish more objective criteria for funding. Institutions are allowed to use their complete subsidies as they deem necessary, may also seek outside sources of funding to complement the state contributions, and may establish profit-making activities.
- Performance contracts, first introduced in 1999, serve as a type of contract between the government and an individual institution regarding how that institution will seek to maximize its individual strengths.

Institutions work to their strengths, as defined by themselves, and seek successes at points where they are most competitive.

Institutional Leadership

- Leadership at every level is balanced within and outside.
- Governance of the institution is primarily in the purview of an external majority university board whose members are elected, not appointed, and include representatives from both within and outside the university, including academic and administrative staff and students.
- Each university's rector serves at the will of the board.
- Deans are hired and supervised by the rector and in turn hire and supervise department heads.

Source: University Act of 2003, retrieved on December 14, 2005, from http://en.vtu.dk/acts/act-on-universities/act-on-universities.pdf.

Recent Research Excellence Initiatives

Country/region	Name of initiative	Number of target institutions and eligibility criteria	Resources allocated	Investment horizon
Africa	NEPAD/Blair Commission for Africa (proposed)[a]	Revitalize Africa's institutions of higher education. Develop centers of excellence in science and technology, including African institutes of technology	US$500 million a year, over 10 years; Up to US$3 billion over 10 years	Launched in 2006
Canada	Canada Networks of Centers of Excellence[b]	23 currently funded Networks of Centers of Excellence; 16 previously funded Networks	C$77.4 million per year since 1999; C$47.3 million a year in 1997–99; C$437 million in total in 1988–98	Operating since 1988; permanent program since 1997
Canada	Canada Global Excellence Research Chairs[c]	Four priorities in the Federal Science and Technology Strategy: the environment, natural resources and energy, health, and information and communication technologies	C$21 million	2009–12
Chile	Chile Millennium Science Initiative[d]	Groups of researchers	3 science institutes: US$1 million a year for 10 years; 5–12 science nuclei: US$250,000 a year; US$25 million in total in 2000–04	Every 5 years for nuclei and every 10 years for institutes

China	China 211 Project[e]	107 higher-education institutions	Y 36.82 billion during 1995–2005	Launched in 1996: 1996–2000 (1st round) 2001–06 (2nd round) 2007–11(3rd round)
China	China 985 Project[f]	39 research universities	Y 27.07 billion (1st round)	Launched in 1999: 1999–2001 (1st round) 2004–07 (2nd round)
China	Chinese Academy of Sciences (CAS) Institutes[g]	Mathematics and physics 15 Chemistry and chemical engineering 12 Biological sciences 20 Earth sciences 19 Technological sciences 21 Others 2	Y 4.80 billion (1st round)	1998–2000 (1st round) 2001–05 (2nd round) 2006–10 (3rd round)
Denmark	Denmark (Globalization Fund)	Funds to be allocated to research universities on a competitive basis	US$1.9 billion between 2007 and 2012	Launched in 2006
Europe	European Commission, Framework Programme 7 (FP7)[h]	TBD – determined by structure of research proposals (RFPs)	Based on number of RFPs with a "center of excellence" structure Overall FP7 budget is €50.5 billion covering 2007–13[i]	2007–13
France	"Opération Campus"[j]	Develop 10 regional centers of excellence in higher education and research. Overall, the centers will regroup 38 universities and research organizations, representing 340,000 students and 13,000 researchers.	€5 billion	Launched in 2008

(continued)

Country/ region	Name of initiative	Number of target institutions and eligibility criteria	Resources allocated	Investment horizon
Germany	Germany Excellence Initiative 2006[k]	40 graduate schools; 30 clusters of excellence (universities and private sector); 10 top-level research universities	US$2.3 billion in tota[l]	Five-year funding; two rounds: 2006 and 2007
Japan	Japan Top-30 Program (Centers Of Excellence for 21st-Century Plan)[l]	31 higher-education institutions	US$150 million/year,program total: 37.8 billion yen)	Five-year funding; launched in 2002; 3 rounds: 2002, 2003, and 2004
Japan	Japan Global Centers of Excellence Program[m]	50–75 centers funded per year (5 new fields of study each year)	50 million–500 million yen per center per year (~US$400,000–US$4 million)	5 years; launched in 2007
Republic of Korea	Brain Korea 21 Program[n]	Science and technology: 11 universities; Humanities and social sciences: 11 universities; Leading regional universities: 38 universities; Professional graduate schools in 11 universities	US$1.17 billion in total	7 years; two rounds in 1999
Republic of Korea	Korea Science and Engineering Foundation (KOSEF)[o]	Science research centers (SRCs)/ engineering research centers (ERCs): up to 65 centers	US$64.2 million/year	1) up to 9 years 2) up to 9 years 3) up to 7 years

		Medical science and engineering research centers (MRCs): 18 centers National core research centers (NCRCs); 6 centers funded in 2006	US$7 million/year US$10.8 million/year	All 3 programs launched in FY 2002 or FY 2003
Russian Federation	Russian Federation's "Federal Universities"[p]	Establish a network of high-status federal institutions that are specialized research universities and lifelong vocational centers	n.a.	Under consideration (two pilot universities were established in 2007)
Taiwan (China)	Taiwan Development Plan for University-Selection and financial sity Research Excellence[q] support of internationally leading fields		US$400 million	4 years
United Kingdom	U.K. Funding for Excellent Units[r]	Universities with the highest marks after the research assessment exercise (RAE)	US$8.63 billion disbursed after 2001 RAE	5 years for research council–funded centers[s] Two rounds: 1996 and 2001; 2008 RAE scheduled[t]
United States, Arizona	Science Foundation Arizona[u]	Public-private partnership to strengthen scientific, engineering, and medical research	US$135 million + US$135 million (1:1 matching)	Annually since 2006
United States, California	California Institutes of Science and Innovation[v]	University-industry partnerships to address state problems	US$400 million + US$800 million (2:1 matching)	Annually since 2000

(continued)

Country/region	Name of initiative	Number of target institutions and eligibility criteria	Resources allocated	Investment horizon
United States, North Dakota	North Dakota Centers of Excellence[w]	Public-private centers focusing on local needs	US$50 million + US$100 million (2:1 matching)	Annually since 2007
United States, Washington	Washington State Life Sciences Discovery Fund[x]	Bioscience research that provides economic and health benefits	US$350 million	10 years since 2005
United States, Georgia	Georgia Research Alliance[y]	Public-private partnership to recruit eminent scholars to Georgia universities	US$30 million	Annually since 1990
United States, Indiana	Indiana 21st-Century Research and Technology Fund[z]	Academic and commercial sector partnerships	US$26 million	Annually since 1999
United States, Kentucky	Kentucky's "Buck for Brains"[aa]	Endowed chairs for top talent	US$350 million	Since 1997
United States, Ohio	Ohio's Third Frontier[bb]	Establishment of centers of innovation as joint initiatives of universities and private research organizations	US$1.6 billion	10 years since 2003
United States, Oklahoma	Oklahoma Center for the Advancement of Science and Technology[cc]	Nanotechnology research	US$29 million	Annually since 1987

Sources: Produced by Natalia Agapitova, Alka Arora, Michael Ehst, and Jamil Salmi (last update June 23, 2008).

Note: US$ = U.S. dollars, C$ = Canadian dollars, Y = Chinese yuan, € = euros, n.a. = not available.

a. http://www.eurodad.org/articles/default.aspx?id=595.

b. http://www.nce.gc.ca/.

c. www.budget.gc.ca/2008/speech-discours/speech-discours-eng.asp.

d. http://www.msi-sig.org/msi/current.html.

e. Ministerial Office of 211 Project (2007), *Report on 211 Project (1995–2005)*. Beijing: Higher Education Press.

f. N. C. Liu and L. Zhou (2007), *Building Research University for Achieving the Goal of an Innovative Country*. Beijing: China Renmin University Press.

g. http://www.itps.se/Archive/Documents/Swedish/Publikationer/Rapporter/Arbetsrapporter%20(R)/R2007/R2007_001%20FoU-finansiarer.pdf. Chinese Academy of Science, http://www.cas.ac.cn/html/books/o6122/e1/04/tongzhi/tz004.htm; http://baike.baidu.com/view/229786.htm.

h. http://ec.europa.eu/research/era/pdf/centres.pdf.

i. http://cordis.europa.eu/fp7/what_en.html#funding.

j. http://www.france-science.org/Operation-Campus-6-projects-kept?var_recherche=operation%20campus; http://www.universityworldnews.com/article.php?story=2008061309292742.

k. http://www.dfg.de/en/research_funding/coordinated_programmes/excellence_initiative/.

l. http://www.jsps.go.jp/english/e-21coe/index.html.

m. http://www.jsps.go.jp/english/e-globalcoe/index.html; http://www.jsps.go.jp/english/e-globalcoe/data/application_guidelines.pdf; http://www.jsps.go.jp/english/e-globalcoe/data/review_guidelines.pdf.

n. http://unpan1.un.org/intradoc/groups/public/documents/APCITY/UNPAN015416.pdf; http://www.bk21.or.kr/datas/english_ver.htm.

o. http://www.kosef.re.kr/english_new/programs/programs_01_04.html.

p. http://www.universityworldnews.com/article.php?story=20081024094454199.

q. http://unpan1.un.org/intradoc/groups/public/documents/APCITY/UNPAN015416.pdf.

r. http://www.hefce.ac.uk/research/funding/.

s. http://www.rcuk.ac.uk/research/resfunding.htm.

t. http://www.rae.ac.uk/.

u. http://www.sfaz.org/.

v. http://www.ucop.edu/california-institutes/about/about.htm.

w. http://governor.state.nd.us/media/speeches/040325.html.

x. http://www.lsdfa.org/home.html.

y. http://www.gra.org/homepage.asp.

z. http://www.21fund.org/.

aa. http://www.wku.edu/IA/bucks/index.html.

bb. http://www.odod.ohio.gov/tech/program.htm.

cc. http://www.ocast.state.ok.us/.

The Best by Any Measure, 2007–08

SJTU 2008 ranking	THES 2008 ranking	University[i]	Annual expenditures (US$)	Student enrollment	Expenditures per student (US$)
1	1	Harvard University[a,b] (United States)	$3,170,650,000	29,900	$106,041.81
2	17	Stanford University[c] (United States)	$3,265,800,000	19,782	$165,089.48
3	36	University of California, Berkeley (United States)	$1,700,000,000	32,910	$51,656.03
4	3	University of Cambridge[d] (United Kingdom)	$1,470,940,000	25,465	$57,763.20
5	9	Massachusetts Institute of Technology (MIT)[m] (United States)	$2,207,600,000	10,220	$216,007.83
6	5	California Institute of Technology[e] (United States)	$2,287,291,000	2,245	$1,018,837.86
7	10	Columbia University[g] (United States)	$2,690,000,000	23,709	$113,459.02
8	12	Princeton University[f] (United States)	$1,196,570,000	6,708	$178,379.55
9	8	University of Chicago[h] (United States)	$1,497,700,000	14,962	$100,100.25
10	4	University of Oxford[l] (United Kingdom)	$1,081,350,000	23,620	$45,781.12
11	2	Yale University (United States)	$2,100,000,000	11,851	$177,200.24
19	19	University of Tokyo[n] (Japan)*	$2,286,974,741	29,347	$77,928.74
24	24	Swiss Federal Institute of Technology (Switzerland)	$1,076,734,500	13,999	$76,915.10
24	41	University of Toronto[j] (Canada)	$1,060,000,000	71,202	$14,887.22
42	149	University of Paris VI (France)	n.a.	30,045	xx
45	48	University of Copenhagen[k] (Denmark)	$1,023,804,249	31,098	$32,921.87
47	67	University of Utrecht (Netherlands)	$925,697,362	27,175	$34,064.30
51	n/a	Karolinska Institute[v] (Sweden)	$550,449,908	7,932	$69,396.11
55	93	University of Munich[l] (Germany)	$501,296,087	22,236	$22,544.35

59	16	Australian National University[p]	$479,665,993	15,869	$30,226.60
64	177	University of Oslo[q] (Norway)	n.a.	27,926	xx
65	93	Hebrew University of Jerusalem[aa] (Israel)	n.a.	23,400	xx
68	91	University of Helsinki[s] (Finland)	$719,230,989	37,975	$18,939.59
70	183	Moscow State University[z] (Russian Federation)	n.a.	47,000	xx
101-51	136	University of Ghent[bb] (Belgium)	$512,674,451	29,553	$17,347.63
101-51	196	University of São Paulo (Brazil)	n.a.	77,307	xx
101-51	n/a	University of Milan[t] (Italy)	$536,407,000	66,120	$8,112.63
101-51	30	National University of Singapore[u]	$1,209,592,000	27,972	$43,242.96
152-200	50	Seoul National University[o] (Republic of Korea)	$940,000,000	29,295	$32,087.39
152-200	197	University of Buenos Aires[x] (Argentina)	n.a.	279,306	xx
152-200	150	National Autonomous University of Mexico (UNAM)[y]	$1,550,431,690	190,418	$8,142.25
201-302	49	Trinity College Dublin[w] (Ireland)*	$348,719,310	13,308	xx
201-302	143	Nanjing University (China)	n.a.	43,477	xx

SJTU 2008 ranking	THES 2008 ranking	University[r]	Faculty size	Enrolled students	Students: faculty	International faculty	International faculty (percentage)
1	1	Harvard University[a,b] (United States)	3,788	29,900	8	1,197	32
2	17	Stanford University[c] (United States)	1,772	19,782	11	92	5
3	36	University of California, Berkeley (United States)	1,736	32,910	19	546	31
4	3	University of Cambridge[d] (United Kingdom)	3,933	25,465	6	1,627	41
5	9	Massachusetts Institute of Technology (MIT)[m] (United States)	1,805	10,220	6	135	7
6	5	California Institute of Technology[e] (United States)	439	2,245	5	341	78
7	10	Columbia University[g] (United States)	3,869	23,709	6	279	7
8	12	Princeton University[f] (United States)	878	6,708	8	312	36
9	8	University of Chicago[h] (United States)	2,797	14,962	5	628	22
10	4	University of Oxford (United Kingdom)	4,197	23,620	6	1,598	38
11	2	Yale University (United States)	2,902	11,851	4	954	33
19	19	University of Tokyo[n] (Japan)	5,615	29,347	5	301	5
24	24	Swiss Federal Institute of Technology (Switzerland)	1,578	13,999	9	821	52
24	41	University of Toronto[j] (Canada)	2,593	71,202	27	728	28
42	149	University of Paris VI (France)	4,647	30,045	6	193	4
45	48	University of Copenhagen[k] (Denmark)	9,680	31,098	3	1,108	11
47	67	University of Utrecht[v] (Netherlands)	3,384	27,175	8	382	11
51	n/a	Karolinska Institute[v] (Sweden)	2,350	7,932	3	301	13
55	93	University of Munich[i] (Germany)	3,527	22,236	6	540	15
59	16	Australian National University[p]	1,556	15,869	10	708	46

64	177	University of Oslo[q] (Norway)	3,248	27,926	9	383	12
65	93	Hebrew University of Jerusalem[aa] (Israel)	1,300	23,400	18	260	20
68	91	University of Helsinki[s] (Finland)	3,147	37,975	12	255	8
70	183	Moscow State University[z] (Russian Federation)	4,000	47,000	12	20	1
101–51	136	University of Ghent[bb] (Belgium)	4,670	29,553	6	460	10
101–51	196	University of São Paulo (Brazil)	5,432	77,307	14	406	7
101–51	n/a	University of Milan[t] (Italy)	3,291	66,120	20	154	5
101–51	30	National University of Singapore[u]	2,416	27,972	12	1,198	50
152–200	50	Seoul National University[o] (Republic of Korea)	5,106	29,295	6	209	4
152–200	197	University of Buenos Aires[x] (Argentina)	24,508	279,306	11	1,249	5
152–200	150	National Autonomous University of México (UNAM)[y]	29,386	190,418	6	2,377	8
201–302	49	Trinity College Dublin[w] (Ireland)	1,552	13,308	9	622	40
201–302	143	Nanjing University (China)	2,728	43,477	16	300	11

Note: n.a. = not applicable, xx = could not be calculated with data available, * = data from 2007.

a. http://www.provost.harvard.edu/institutional_research/factbook.php.

b. http://www.news.harvard.edu/glance/.

c. http://www.stanford.edu/about/facts/faculty.html#profile.

d. http://www.admin.cam.ac.uk/reporter/2007-08/weekly/6099/4.html.

e. http://www.caltech.edu/at-a-glance/.

f. http://www.princeton.edu/main/about/facts/.

g. http://www.columbia.edu/cu/opir/facts.html.

h. http://www.uchicago.edu/about/documents/.

i. http://www.ox.ac.uk/about_the_university/facts_and_figures/index.html.

j. http://www.utoronto.com/aboutuoft/quickfacts.htm.

k. http://facts.ku.dk/finance/income/.

l. http://www.en.uni-muenchen.de/about_lmu/factsfigs/index.html.

m. http://web.mit.edu/facts/financial.html.

n. http://www.u-tokyo.ac.jp/fin01/b06_01_e.html.

o. http://www.useoul.edu/about/ab0103.jsp.

p. http://unistats.anu.edu.au/.

q. http://universitas.no/news/.

r. http://www.nacubo.org/.

s. http://www.helsinki.fi/vuosikertomus2007/english/keyfigures/index.htm.

t. http://www.unimi.it/ENG/university/29502.htm#c32697.

u. http://www.nus.edu.sg/annualreport/2007/financial_summary.htm.

v. http://ki.se/ki/jsp/polopoly.jsp?d=130&l=sv.

w. http://www.tcd.ie/Treasurers_Office/gen_finstats.php.

x. http://www.uba.ar/ingles/about/index.php.

y. http://www.planeacion.unam.mx/agenda/2007/.

z. http://www.msu.ru/en/.

aa. http://www.huji.ac.il/huji/eng/.

bb. http://www.ugent.be/en/ghentuniv/report.

Bibliography

On World-Class Universities

Aghion, P., M. Dewatripont, C. Hoxby, A. Mas-Colell, and A. Sapir. 2007. "Why Reform Europe's Universities?" Policy Brief 2007/04, Bruegel, Brussels.

———. 2008. "Higher Aspirations: An Agenda for Reforming European Universities." Vol. V, Blueprint Series, Bruegel, Brussels. Retrieved December 2, 2008, from http://www.bmwf.gv.at/fileadmin/user_upload/europa/bologna/BPJULY2008University_1_.pdf.

Alden, J., and G. Lin. 2004. "Benchmarking the Characteristics of a World-Class University: Developing an International Strategy at University Level." Leadership Foundation for Higher Education, London.

Altbach, Philip G. 2003. "The Costs and Benefits of World-Class Universities: An American's Perspective." Hong Kong America Center, Chinese University of Hong Kong, Hong Kong, China.

———. 2004. "The Costs and Benefits of World-Class Universities." *Academe* 90 (1, January-February). Retrieved April 10, 2006, from http://www.aaup.org/AAUP/pubsres/academe/2004/JF/Feat/altb.htm.

———. 2005. "A World-Class Country without World-Class Higher Education: India's 21st Century Dilemma." *International Higher Education* (40, Summer): 18–20. Retrieved April 10, 2007, from http://www.bc.edu/bc_org/avp/soe/cihe/newsletter/ihe_pdf/ihe40.pdf.

Bradshaw, D. 2007. "India's Elite Schools Aim at Autonomy." *Financial Times*, October 14.

Brown, Susan. 2007. "China Challenges the West in Stem-Cell Research: Unconstrained by Public Debate, Cities Like Shanghai and Beijing Lure Scientists with New Laboratories and Grants." *Chronicle of Higher Education* 53 (32, April 13): A14–A18.

BusinessWeek. 2007. "The Dangerous Wealth of the Ivy League." *BusinessWeek* (November 29). Retrieved December 3, 2008, from http://www.business week.com/magazine/content/07_50/b4062038784589.htm.

Carey, K. 2007. "America's Best Community Colleges: Why They're Better Than Some of the 'Best' Four-Year Universities." *Washington Monthly* (June). Retrieved July 18, 2008, from http://www.washingtonmonthly.com/features/ 2007/ 0709.careyessay.html.

Csikszentmihalyi, M. 1997. *Creativity: Flow and the Psychology of Discovery and Invention*. New York: HarperCollins.

Deem, R., K. H. Mok, and L. Lucas. 2008. "Transforming Higher Education in Whose Image? Exploring the Concept of the 'World-Class' University in Europe and Asia." *Higher Education Policy* 21 (1): 83–97.

Donoghue, S., and M. Kennerley. Forthcoming. "Our Journey Towards World Class: Leading Transformational Strategic Change." *Higher Education Management and Policy*.

Economist. 2005. "Secrets of Success." *Economist* 376 (8443, September 8): 6. Retrieved December 2, 2008, from http://www.economist.com/surveys/ displaystory.cfm?story_id=E1_QPPJJQQ.

French, Howard W. 2005. "China Luring Foreign Scholars to Make Its Universities Great." *New York Times*, October 28.

Goodall, A. 2006. "The Leaders of the World's Top 100 Universities." *International Higher Education* (42, Winter): 3–4. Retrieved December 2, 2008, from http://www.bc.edu/bc_org/avp/soe/cihe/newsletter/ihe_pdf/ihe42.pdf.

Harman, G., and K. Harman. 2008. "Strategic Mergers of Strong Institutions to Enhance Competitive Advantage." *Higher Education Policy* 21 (1): 99–121.

Hatakenaka, S. 2007. "Culture of Innovation: Lessons from International Experience." Unpublished paper, Massachusetts Institute of Technology (MIT).

Kahn, A., and V. Malingre. 2007. "*Les* French economists *font école*." *Le Monde*, February 22, 3.

Kehm, B. 2006. "The German 'Initiative for Excellence' and the Issue of Ranking." *International Higher Education* (44, Summer). Retrieved December 2, 2008, from http://www.bc.edu/bc_org/avp/soe/cihe/newsletter/ihe_pdf/ihe44.pdf.

Khoon, K. A., R. Shukor, O. Hassan, Z. Saleh, A. Hamzah, and R. Ismail. 2005. "Hallmark of a World-Class University." *College Student Journal* (December).

Retrieved April 10, 2007, from http://findarticles.com/p/articles/mi_m0FCR/is_4_39/ai_n16123684.

Kuznetsov, Y., ed. 2006. *Diaspora Networks and the International Migration of Skills: How Countries Can Draw on Their Talent Abroad*. Washington, DC: World Bank.

Levin, M. H., D. W. Jeong, and D. Ou. 2006. "What is a World Class University?" Paper prepared for the Conference of the Comparative and International Education Society, Honolulu, HI, March 16. Retrieved April 12, 2007, from www.tc.columbia.edu/centers/coce/pdf_files/c12.pdf.

McNeill, D. 2007. "Japan's New Science Adviser Wants to Shake Up Higher Education." *Chronicle of Higher Education* 53 (39, June 1): A37. Retrieved July 15, 2008, from http://chronicle.com/daily/2007/05/2007052508n.htm.

Miller, R. 2007a. "Beyond Study Abroad: Preparing Engineers for the New Global Economy." Unpublished paper, Olin College of Engineering, Needham, MA.

———. 2007b. "Observations on Efforts to Create a New Paradigm for Undergraduate Education in Engineering." Reported in a case study published by the Harvard Macy Institute and the President and Fellows of Harvard College, Cambridge, MA.

Mohrman, Kathryn. 2003. "Higher Education Reform in Mainland Chinese Universities: An American's Perspective." Hong Kong America Center, Chinese University of Hong Kong, Hong Kong, China.

Neelakantan, S. 2007. "In India, Economic Success Leaves Universities Desperate for Professors." *Chronicle of Higher Education* 54 (7, October 12): A37–A38. Retrieved December 11, 2008, from http://chronicle.com/weekly/v54/i07/07a03701.htm.

Niland, J. 2000. "The Challenge of Building World Class Universities in the Asian Region." *ON LINE Opinion* (February 3). Retrieved April 10, 2006, from http://www.onlineopinion.com.au/view.asp?article=997.

———. 2007. "The Challenge of Building World-Class Universities." In *The World Class University and Ranking: Aiming Beyond Status*, ed. J. Sadlak and N. C. Liu. Bucharest: UNESCO-CEPES.

Orivel, F. 2004. *"Pourquoi les universités françaises sont-elles si mal classées dans les palmarès internationaux?" Dijon: Notes de l'IREDU* (May).

Qureshi, Yakub. 2007. "400 University Jobs Could Go." *Manchester Evening News*, March 9. Retrieved May 20, 2007, from http://www.manchestereveningnews.co.uk/news/education/s/1001/1001469_400_university_jobs_could_go.html.

Schwartz, J. 2007. "Reengineering Engineering: The Hands-On Approach: Building a Different Breed of Engineer at Olin College." *New York Times Magazine*, September 30. Retrieved December 3, 2008, from http://www.nytimes.com/2007/09/30/magazine/30OLIN-t.html?_r=1&scp=1&sq=Olin+college&st=nyt.

Schwartzman, Simon. 2005. "Brazil's Leading University: Between Intelligentsia, World Standards and Social Inclusion." Instituto de Estudos do Trabalho e Sociedade, Rio de Janeiro, Brazil. Retrieved December 2, 2008, from http://www.schwartzman.org.br/simon/worldclasss.pdf.

Simmons, Ruth. 2003. "How to Make a World-Class University." *South China Morning Post*, January 18. Hong Kong, China.

THES (Times Higher Education Supplement). 2006. "Dons Urged to Reject Reforms." *THES* (November 14). Retrieved December 2, 2008, from http://www.timeshighereducation.co.uk/story.asp?storyCode=206746&sectioncode=26.

University of Auckland. 2007. "Commentary on Issues of Higher Education and Research." Office of the Vice-Chancellor, University of Auckland, New Zealand (Issue 1, August). Retrieved December 2, 2008, from http://www.auckland.ac.nz/uoa/fms/default/uoa/about/commentary/docs/commentary_issue_1.pdf.

Usher, A. 2006. "Can Our Schools Become World-Class?" *Globe and Mail*, Toronto, October 30. Retrieved December 2, 2008, from http://www.theglobeandmail.com/servlet/story/RTGAM.20061030.URCworldclassp28/BNStory/univreport06/home.

Yusuf, S., and K. Nabeshima. 2007. *How Universities Promote Economic Growth*. Washington DC: World Bank.

On the Knowledge Economy and the Role of Tertiary Education

Cookson, C. 2007. "Universities Drive Biotech Advancement." *Financial Times Europe*, May 7, 3.

Gibbons, M., C. Limoges, H. Nowotny, S. Schwartzman, P. Scott, and M. Trow. 1994. *The New Production of Knowledge: Science and Research in Contemporary Societies*. London: SAGE.

NAE (National Academy of Engineering). 2005. *Educating the Engineer of 2020: Adapting Engineering Education to the New Century*. Washington, DC: National Academies Press.

Perry, N., and D. Sherlock. 2008. *Quality Improvement in Adult Vocational Education and Training: Transforming Skills for the Global Economy*. London: Kogan Page.

Saint, William. 2006. "Innovation Funds for Higher Education: A User's Guide for World Bank Funded Projects." Education Working Paper 1, World Bank, Washington, DC. Retrieved July 15, 2008, from http://go.worldbank.org/FW6F3AMW30.

World Bank. 1994. *Higher Education: Lessons of Experience*. Washington, DC: World Bank.

————. 1999a. *World Development Report 1998/99: Knowledge for Development.* Washington, DC: World Bank. Retrieved December 2, 2008, from http://www.worldbank.org/wdr/wdr98/contents.htm.

————. 1999b. *World Development Report 1999/2000: Entering the 21st Century.* Washington, DC: World Bank. Retrieved December 2, 2008, from http://www.worldbank.org/wdr/2000/fullreport.html.

————. 2002. *Constructing Knowledge Societies: New Challenges for Tertiary Education.* Washington, DC: World Bank. Retrieved December 2, 2008, from http://go.worldbank.org/N2QADMBNI0.

On Rankings

Bougnol, M.-L., and Dulá, J. H. 2006. "Validating DEA as a Ranking Tool: An Application of DEA to Assess Performance in Higher Education." *Annals of Operations Research* 145 (1, July): 339–65.

Bowden, R. 2000. "Fantasy Higher Education: University and College League Tables." *Quality in Higher Education* 6 (1, April 1): 41–60.

Brooks, R. L. 2005. "Measuring University Quality." *Review of Higher Education* 29 (1, Fall): 1–21.

Clarke, M. 2002. "Some Guidelines for Academic Quality Rankings." *Higher Education in Europe* 27 (4): 443–59.

————. 2005. "Quality Assessment Lessons from Australia and New Zealand." *Higher Education in Europe* 30 (2, July): 183–97.

Diamond, N., and H. D. Graham. 2000. "How Should We Rate Research Universities?" *Change* 32 (4, July/August): 20–33.

Dill, D., and M. Soo. 2005. "Academic Quality, League Tables, and Public Policy: A Cross-National Analysis of University Ranking Systems." *Higher Education,* 49 (4, June): 495–533.

Eccles, C. 2002. "The Use of University Rankings in the United Kingdom." *Higher Education in Europe* 27 (4): 423–32.

Filinov, N. B., and S. Ruchkina. 2002. "The Ranking of Higher Education Institutions in Russia: Some Methodological Problems." *Higher Education in Europe* 27 (4): 407–21.

Goddard, A. 1999. "League Tables May End in Tiers." *Times Higher Education Supplement* (1371, February 12): 1.

IHEP (Institute for Higher Education Policy), ed. 2007. *College and University Ranking Systems: Global Perspectives and American Challenges.* Washington, DC: IHEP. Retrieved December 2, 2008, from http://www.ihep.org/assets/files/publications/a-f/CollegeRankingSystems.pdf.

Jobbins, D. 2005. "Moving to a Global Stage: A Media View." *Higher Education in Europe* 30 (2, July): 137–45.

Liu, N. C., and Y. Cheng. 2005. "The Academic Ranking of World Universities: Methodologies and Problems." *Higher Education in Europe* 30 (2, July): 127–36.

Liu, N. C., and L. Liu. 2005. "University Rankings in China." *Higher Education in Europe* 30 (2, July): 217–28.

Marshall, Jane. 2008. "France: Universities Lag 'Digitally Native' Students." *University World News*, August 10. Retrieved December 2, 2008, from http://www.universityworldnews.com/article.php?story=20080807153500208.

Monks, J., and R. G. Ehrenberg. 1999. "*U.S. News & World Report's* College Rankings: Why They Do Matter." *Change* 31 (6, November-December): 42–51.

Pace, C. R., and D. G. Wallace. 1954. "Evaluation of Institutional Programs." *Review of Educational Research* 24 (4, October): 341–50.

Print, M., and J. Hattie. 1997. "Measuring Quality in Universities: An Approach to Weighting Research Productivity." *Higher Education* 33 (4, June): 453–69.

Provan, D., and K. Abercromby. 2000. "University League Tables and Rankings: A Critical Analysis." Paper No. 30, Commonwealth Higher Education Management Service (CHEMS), London. Retrieved December 3, 2008, from http://www.acu.ac.uk/chems/onlinepublications/976798333.pdf.

QS (Quacquarelli Symonds). 2008. "The Methodology: A Simple Overview." *Top Universities*. Retrieved December 11, 2008, from http://www.topuniversities.com/worlduniversityrankings/methodology/simple_overview/.

Ramsden, P. 1998. *Learning to Lead in Higher Education*. London and New York: Routledge.

Rocki, M. 2005. "Statistical and Mathematical Aspects of Ranking: Lessons from Poland." *Higher Education in Europe* 30 (2, July): 173–81.

Salmi, J., and A. Saroyan. 2007. "League Tables as Policy Instruments: Uses and Misuses." *Higher Education Management and Policy* 19 (2): 24–62.

Shultziner, D. 2008. "Nightmare in Dreaming Spires." *Guardian*, April 29.

SJTU (Shanghai Jiao Tong University). 2008. *Academic Ranking of World Universities 2008*. Retrieved September 30, 2008, from http://www.arwu.org/rank2008/EN2008.htm.

SLATE. 2003–05. "Organizational History." Retrieved March 13, 2006, from http://www.slatearchives.org/orghist.htm.

Stuart, D. 1995. "Reputational Rankings: Background and Development." *New Directions for Institutional Research* 1995 (88, Winter): 13–20.

Stuit, D. 1960. "Evaluations of Institutions and Programs." *Review of Educational Research* 30 (4): 371–84.

THES. 2008. *The Times Higher Education World University Rankings 2008*. Retrieved September 30, 2008, from http://www.timeshighereducation.co.uk/hybrid.asp?typeCode=243&pubCode=1.

Turner, D. R. 2005. "Benchmarking in Universities: League Tables Revisited." *Oxford Review of Education* 31 (3, September): 353–71.

U.S. News & World Report. 2008. "America's Best Graduate Schools." Retrieved June 10, 2008, from http://grad-schools.usnews.rankingsandreviews.com/grad.

———. 2009. "Best Colleges 2009: National Universities Ranking." Retrieved January 14, 2009, from http://colleges.usnews.rankingsandreviews.com/college/national-search.

Usher, A., and M. Savino. 2006. "A World of Difference: A Global Survey of University League Tables." Canadian Education Report Series, Education Policy Institute, Toronto, Ontario. Retrieved December 3, 2008, from http://www.eric.ed.gov/ERICDocs/data/ericdocs2sql/content_storage_01/0000019b/80/3c/85/46.pdf.

Van Dyke, N. 2005. "Twenty Years of University Report Cards." *Higher Education in Europe* 30 (2, July): 103–25.

Williams, R., and N. Van Dyke. 2007. "Measuring the International Standing of Universities with an Application to Australian Universities." *Higher Education* 53 (6, June): 819–41.

Winston, G. C., and D. J. Zimmerman. 2003. "Peer Effects in Higher Education." Working Paper 9501, National Bureau of Economic Research (NBER), Cambridge, MA. Retrieved May 10, 2006, from http://www.nber.org/papers/w9501.

Statistical Sources and Country Documents

CHE (Chronicle of Higher Education). 2006. "The 2006–7 Almanac." Retrieved December 11, 2008 from http://chronicle.com/free/almanac/2006/index.htm.

———. 2007. "Special Report: Executive Compensation." *Chronicle of Higher Education* 53 (13, November 16): B1–B9.

Durham, E. 2008. "Fábricas de maus professors." *Veja.* November 28.

EC (European Commission). 2007. *Remuneration of Researchers in the Public and Private Sectors.* Research Directorate–General. Brussels: EC Publications. Retrieved December 3, 2008, from http://ec.europa.eu/euraxess/pdf/final_report.pdf.

Economist. 2006. "Lessons from the Campus." Special Survey Section on France. *Economist* (October 28).

Egide. 2007. "Special Report by the Egide Association: *Les enjeux de la mobilité.*" Retrieved June 7, 2007, from http://www.egide.asso.fr/fr/services/actualites/lettre/L34/dossier34.jhtml.

Gupta, Asha. 2008. "Caste, Class, and Quality at the Indian Institutes of Technology." *International Higher Education* (53, Fall): 20–21. Retrieved December 3, 2008, from http://www.bc.edu/bc_org/avp/soe/cihe/newslet ter/ihe_pdf/ihe53.pdf.

Holdsworth, N. 2008. "Russia: Super League of 'Federal' Universities." *University World News,* October 26. Retrieved December 3, 2008, from http://www.universityworldnews.com/article.php?story=20081024094454199.

Jan, T. 2008. "Colleges Scour China for Top Students." *The Boston Globe*, November 9. Retrieved December 2, 2008, from http://www.boston.com/news/education/higher/articles/2008/11/09/colleges_scour_china_for_top_students/

Jardine, D. 2008. "Malaysia: Inter-ethnic Tensions Touch Universities." *University World News*, August 31. Retrieved December 3, 2008, from http://www.universityworldnews.com/article.php?story=2008082814421654.

Mangan, K. 2008. "Cornell Graduates the Inaugural Class at Its Medical College in Qatar." *Chronicle of Higher Education* 54 (36, May 16): A28. Retrieved July 15, 2008, from http://chronicle.com/daily/2008/05/2754n.htm.

NACUBO (National Association of College and University Business Officers). 2006. "University Fundraising: An Update." Retrieved April 30, 2008, from http://www.suttontrust.com/reports/UniversityFundraisingDec06.pdf.

Nature. 2008. "The EIT Farce." *Nature* 452 (254, March 20). Retrieved December 3, 2008, from http://www.nature.com/nature/journal/v452/n7185/full/452254b.html.

Normile, D. 2006. "Singapore-Hopkins Partnership Ends in a Volley of Fault-Finding." *Science* 313 (5787, August 4): 600.

OECD. 2007. *Education at a Glance 2007*. Paris: OECD. Retrieved December 3, 2008, from http://www.oecd.org/document/30/0,3343,en_2649_39263238_39251550_1_1_1_1,00.html.

———. 2009. *Reviews of National Policies for Education: Tertiary Education in Chile 2008*. Paris and Washington, DC: OECD and World Bank.

Tierney, W., and M. Sirat. 2008. "Challenges Facing Malaysian Higher Education." *International Higher Education* (53, Fall): 23–24. Retrieved December 3, 2008, from http://www.bc.edu/bc_org/avp/soe/cihe/newsletter/ihe_pdf/ihe53.pdf.

UNESCO (United Nations Educational, Scientific, and Cultural Organization). 2006. *Global Education Digest 2006: Comparing Education Statistics across the World*. UNESCO Institute for Statistics (UIS). Montreal: UIS. Retrieved December 3, 2008, from http://www.uis.unesco.org/TEMPLATE/pdf/ged/2006/GED2006.pdf.

Universities UK. 2007. "Talent Wars: The International Market for Academic Staff." Policy Briefing (July), Universities UK, London. Retrieved December 3, 2008, from http://www.universitiesuk.ac.uk/Publications/Bookshop/Documents/Policy%20Brief%20Talent%20Wars.pdf.

UWN (University World News). 2008a. "CHINA: Growing Competition for Top Students." *University World News*, June 8. Retrieved June 14, 2008, from http://www.universityworldnews.com/article.php?story=20080605155512411.

———. 2008b. "UK: Oxford's New Vice-Chancellor." *University World News*, June 8. Retrieved June 14, 2008, from http://www.universityworldnews.com/article.php?story=20080606083104456.

Wilson, R. 2008. "Wisconsin's Flagship Campus Is Raided for Scholars." *Chronicle of Higher Education*, 54 (32, April 18): A1, A19, and A25. Retrieved December 3, 2008, from http://chronicle.texterity.com/chroniclesample/20080418-sample/?pg=19.

Index

Boxes, figures, and tables are indicated by *b*, *f*, and *t*, respectively.
Individual universities will be found under the major element in the name rather than at
U for university (e.g., Buenos Aires, University of).

ECO-AUDIT
Environmental Benefits Statement

The World Bank is committed to preserving endangered forests and natural resources. The Office of the Publisher has chosen to print *The Challenge of Establishing World-Class Universities* on recycled paper with 30 percent post-consumer waste, in accordance with the recommended standards for paper usage set by the Green Press Initiative, a nonprofit program supporting publishers in using fiber that is not sourced from endangered forests. For more information, visit www.greenpressinitiative.org.

Saved:
- 7 trees
- 5 million Btus of total energy
- 607 lb. of net greenhouse gases
- 2,520 gallons of waste water
- 324 lb. of solid waste